Basic Skills for the TOEFL® iBT

Edaan Getzel
Tanya Yaunish

Compass
Publishing

Speaking

Basic Skills for the TOEFL® iBT 3
Speaking

Edaan Getzel · Tanya Yaunish

© 2008 Compass Publishing

Project Editor: Liana Robinson
Acquisitions Editor: Emily Page
Content Editor: Erik Custer
Copy Editor: Alice Wrigglesworth
Contributing Writer: Caroline Murphy
Consultants: Lucy Han, Chanhee Park
Cover/Interior Design: Dammora Inc

email: info@compasspub.com
http://www.compasspub.com

ISBN: 978-1-59966-160-5

10 9 8 7 6 5 4 3
10 09

Contents

Introduction to the TOEFL® iBT

What is the TOEFL® test?

The TOEFL® iBT (Test of English as a Foreign Language Internet-based Test) is designed to assess English proficiency in non-native speakers who want to achieve academic success as well as effective communication. It is not meant to test academic knowledge or computer ability; therefore, questions are always based on material found in the test.

The TOEFL® iBT test is divided into four sections:
- Reading
- Speaking
- Listening
- Writing

TOEFL® Scores

TOEFL® scores can be used for:
- Admission into university or college where instruction is in English
- Employers or government agencies who need to determine a person's English ability
- English-learning institutes that need to place students in the appropriate level of English instruction

It is estimated that about 4,400 universities and other institutions require a certain TOEFL® test score for admission.

The exact calculation of a TOEFL® test score is complicated and not necessary for the student to understand. However, it is helpful to know that:
- Each section in the Internet-based test is worth 30 points
- The highest possible score on the iBT is 120 points
- Each institution will have its own specific score requirements

✷ It is very important to check with each institution individually to find out what its admission requirements are.

Registering for the TOEFL® iBT

Students who wish to take the TOEFL® test must get registration information. Registration information can be obtained online at the ETS website. The Internet address is www.ets.org/toefl.

The website provides information such as:
- testing locations
- identification requirements
- registration information
- costs
- other test preparation material
- test center locations

This information will vary depending on the country in which you take the test. Be sure to follow the requirements carefully. If you do not have the proper requirements in order, you may not be able to take the test. Remember that if you register online, you will need to have your credit card information ready.

Introduction to the Speaking Section of the TOEFL® iBT

The purpose of the speaking section is to evaluate your ability to speak coherently on your opinions and experiences as well as on information that you have read or heard.

The speaking questions fall into two categories: independent and integrated.

The prompts for speaking questions on the TOEFL® iBT can be categorized into three types:

Question	Time			
	Reading	Listening	Preparation	Speaking
Independent Q1	---	---	15 seconds	45 seconds
Independent Q2				
Integrated Q3	45 seconds	1-2 minutes	30 seconds	60 seconds
Integrated Q4				
Integrated Q5	---	1-2 minutes	30 seconds	60 seconds
Integrated Q6				

For the two independent speaking questions, you should draw upon your own experiences and knowledge.

For the remaining four speaking questions, you will speak about what you read and/or hear. Your ideas need to be well-organized, and the language you use needs to be accurate enough to be easily understood.

In particular, each question type will require test-takers to organize their ideas and speak toward different goals:

Question	Type	Materials	Description
1	Independent	None	Describe your experience.
2	Independent	None	Give your opinion, and explain why you think this.
3	Integrated	Reading	Restate the opinion of the speaker and the examples used.
		Conversation	
4	Integrated	Reading	Explain how the example from the lecture supports/refutes the reading.
		Lecture	
5	Integrated	Conversation	Restate suggestions, and tell which you think is better.
6	Integrated	Lecture	Summarize what you heard.

How Speaking Will Be Scored

ETS graders will score test-takers' responses according to the following scale:

Score	General Description	Key Points
4	The response answers the question or prompt well. The speaker is easy to understand, and there are only minor mistakes with grammar or pronunciation.	Fluent speech that is easy to understand and follow, appropriate use of grammar and vocabulary, ideas explained clearly
3	The response answers the question or prompt, but not all of the ideas are fully developed. The speaker can be understood, but there are some noticeable mistakes in speaking.	At least two (2) of these problems: pronunciation, pace of speech, wrong word choice, limited use of grammar structures, or incorrect grammar
2	The response gives only a basic or minimal answer to the prompt. Most sentences can be understood, but some effort is required by the listener because speech is not fluent and pronunciation is not accurate. Some ideas are not clearly explained.	At least two (2) of these problems: the speech is choppy (not fluent), there are mistakes in pronunciation, word choice is incorrect, only basic grammar is used, grammar is used poorly, only basic ideas are presented, explanations are absent or limited
1	The response is very short, does not show full understanding of the question or prompt, and is hard for the listener to understand.	At least two (2) of these problems: poor pronunciation is used, speech is choppy (not fluent), there are long or frequent pauses, poor grammar use makes ideas difficult to understand, obviously practiced or formulaic expressions are used, there are many repetitions of expressions in the prompt.
0	There is no response, or the response is not related to the question or prompt.	There is no response to grade, or the response is not related to the question or prompt.

Test management

- You will speak into a microphone attached to a headset.
- Before you begin the speaking section, listen to the headset directions. It is very important that your microphone is working and that your voice can be heard clearly. It is also important that you can hear clearly during the listening section.
- Be aware of time constraints. Check the time with the clock shown in the title bar.
- Independent speaking questions come first.
- Note-taking is permitted. Paper will be provided by the test supervisor. These notes can be studied when preparing your response.
- If you miss something that is said in a conversation or lecture, do not panic. Forget about it, and simply keep listening. Even native speakers do not hear everything that is said.
- You must answer each question as it appears. You can NOT return to any questions later.
- Do not leave any question unanswered. You are NOT penalized for guessing an answer.

Getting Ready to Speak

A. Learn the words.

Key Vocabulary

handy	useful
particularly	specifically; especially
daily planner	a book where people write down their events and meetings
suitable	right for a purpose
fast forward	to skip through or to pass quickly through something

TOEFL® Vocabulary

gadget	a small device that helps to do something
up-to-date	current
commercial	an advertisement on television
tedious	boring or annoying because of length or dullness
irritate	to annoy somebody

B. Read the prompt. Then answer the questions.

Talk about a recent gadget that you saw.

1. Where did you see it?
I saw it _____.

2. What did it do?
The gadget _____.

3. Did it look like it was useful to you? Why?
The gadget _____
because _____.

👤👤 **Now practice the questions and answers with a partner.**

C. **Listen and repeat.** `Track 1-1`

Practice

A. Read the prompt. Then take turns answering the questions with a partner.

Talk about all the different gadgets that you and your family have owned.

1. What is the most expensive gadget your family owns?
2. What is the most useful gadget that your family has?
3. What has been the most disappointing gadget that your family has?
4. Which gadget do you think your family really needs to get?

B. Make a list of descriptive words and phrases to describe gadgets with your classmates.

_____

_____

_____

_____

Prompt 2

C. Read the prompt. Then complete the answers with your own information.

Talk about a useful gadget that you would create.

What?	My gadget would _____.
Why?	I would create this gadget so _____.
Who?	I think _____ would buy this.
Why?	This gadget would be useful because _____ _____.

Now practice your answers with a partner.

D. Make a list of positive descriptive words and phrases about gadgets with a partner.

_____

_____

_____

_____

E. Read the prompt. Then underline the phrases you could use in your own response.

> What is your favorite gadget, and why is it your favorite? Include specific reasons and details in your explanation.

Reasons it is your favorite gadget

- fun to use
- a time saver
- really handy
- is up-to-date
- makes jobs easier
- creates lots of free time

Sample Response and Outline

F. Listen to the sample responses and complete the outlines. `Track 1-2`

Sample response 1		Sample response 2	
_____		_____	
Reason 1	**Reason 2**	**Reason 1**	**Reason 2**
_____	_____	_____	_____
_____	_____	_____	_____
_____	_____	_____	_____
_____	_____	_____	_____
_____	_____	_____	_____

Conclusion: _____

Conclusion: _____

TOEFL® Vocabulary Practice

G. Fill in the blanks with the correct words.

gadgets   up-to-date   commercials   tedious   irritate

1. The newspaper was not _____ because it was three days old.

2. Men tend to like small electronic _____ more than women.

3. Younger brothers and sisters can often _____ their older siblings.

4. Putting lots of letters into lots of envelopes can be very _____ work.

5. People watch the American Super Bowl for both the game and the new _____.

Test

Step 1

Read the prompt.

What is your favorite gadget, and why is it your favorite? Include specific reasons and details in your explanation.

Step 2

Create an outline for your response.

```
        _____
```

Reason 1
_____
_____
_____
_____

Reason 2
_____
_____
_____
_____

Conclusion: _____
_____

Step 3

Write a response using your outline from above.

My favorite gadget is _____.
It has _____
_____
_____.
But most importantly, _____
_____
_____.
I love my _____.

Extension

Work with a partner. Take turns saying your response. Then change partners two more times. Time yourselves!

Your time: _____ seconds	Partner one's time: _____ seconds
Your time: _____ seconds	Partner two's time: _____ seconds
Your time: _____ seconds	Partner three's time: _____ seconds

Integrated

Getting Ready to Speak

A. Learn the words.

medicine	a substance to treat or cure illness
student union	a university building where students can gather
current	now; present time
fever	a high body temperature caused by illness
furious	very angry

physician	a doctor
diagnosis	an analysis of a disease or illness
treatment	something done to help cure an illness or disease
facility	a place of service or convenience
recover	to feel better after an illness or injury

B. Read the announcement. Then answer the questions.

Help Save the Campus Hospital!

The university announced yesterday that it is closing the campus hospital. The university wants to use money they currently spend on the hospital to build a new library. In the future, students will have to see a physician off-campus for injuries and other health problems. Many students rely on the campus hospital for diagnosis and treatment. This will make it more difficult to get important medicine. There will be a meeting in the Student Union on Friday. Please come if you want to help.

1. What will happen?
   The university will _____.

2. Why is the university doing this?
   It is closing it in order to _____.

3. What do you think the conversation will be about?
   I think the conversation will be about _____.

Now practice the questions and answers with a partner.

C. Listen and repeat. `Track 1-3`

Practice

Announcement

A. Read the announcement again and underline the key information.

Help Save the Campus Hospital!

The university announced yesterday that it is closing the campus hospital. The university wants to use money they currently spend on the hospital to build a new library. In the future, students will have to see a physician off-campus for injuries and other health problems. Many students rely on the campus hospital for diagnosis and treatment. This will make it more difficult to get important medicine. There will be a meeting in the Student Union on Friday. Please come if you want to help.

Note-taking

B. Listen to the conversation and take notes. `Track 1-4`

Man	Woman
• Saw _____	• Didn't _____
• The university _____	• The current _____
_____	• A new one would _____
• They want _____	• Could go to _____
• The hospital is _____	• Some are _____
• This one is _____	• Lives _____
• Lives _____	• Will _____
• Doesn't have _____	
• Doesn't want to_____	
• Is _____	
• Going to _____	

Prompt

C. Read the prompt.

The man expresses his opinion of the notice about the university closing the campus hospital. State his opinion, and explain the reasons he gives for holding that opinion.

D. Listen to the sample response and complete the outline. `Track 1-5`

The conversation is about closing the campus hospital so that _____

_____

A. The man is very _____

B. The hospital is

    1. very _____

    2. _____ for students living in the dorms

C. Students will be _____

D. He had to _____

E. He can't go to another hospital because

    1. he doesn't _____

    2. he doesn't want _____

F. He will go _____

Speaking Practice

E. Now work with a partner. Take turns saying your own response using the outline from above.

Your time: _____ seconds   Your partner's time: _____ seconds

TOEFL® Vocabulary Practice

F. Fill in the blanks with the correct words.

diagnosis	facilities	physician	recover	treatments

1. If you are sick, you usually see a _____.

2. There are many _____ at a university.

3. It sometimes takes a long time to _____ from a serious injury.

4. After doing some tests, a doctor can give a patient a _____.

5. Doctors often try a few different _____ to cure an illness.

Test

Step 1

Read the announcement.

> ### New Medical Center Charges
>
> All students should read the following list of current medical center charges. The university did not get enough money from the government this year. As a result, there will now be a cost for seeing a physician. In addition, the price of treatment and medicine has also increased. Everyone must pay these charges. Students who have insurance can get some money back. Please ask a nurse for an insurance form if you need one. Call the number below if you have any questions.

Step 2

Listen to the conversation and take notes. **Track 1-6**

Man	Woman
• Got a copy _____ _____	• Didn't _____
	• Thought the _____
• The university _____	• Went _____
_____	• Has some _____
• Students will have to _____	• But _____
_____	• Thinks there is _____
_____	_____
• Most students _____	• Thinks some _____
• Many people will _____	_____
• Maybe the university will _____	• Is going to _____
_____	

Step 3

Read the prompt.

The woman expresses her opinion about the new medical center charges. State her opinion, and explain the reasons she gives for having that opinion.

Step 4

Create an outline for your response.

The conversation is about the medical center now charging to see a doctor and _____
_____.

A. The woman is _____

B. She went there last week

    1. Got _____

    2. Needs _____

C. The other students will be _____

    1. They may avoid _____

    2. They may get _____

D. There must be another _____

    1. She will _____

    2. She hopes the university will _____

Step 5

Write a response using your outline from above.

The conversation is about _____
_____. The woman is _____.
She went there _____
_____. She is sure the other
students _____, and they may _____.
As a result, many people may _____. She thinks that _____
_____, so
she is going to _____
_____.

Extension

 **Work with a partner. Take turns saying your response. Then change partners
two more times. Time yourselves!**

Your time: _____ seconds   Partner one's time: _____ seconds

Your time: _____ seconds   Partner two's time: _____ seconds

Your time: _____ seconds   Partner three's time: _____ seconds

Check-up

Fill in the blanks with the correct words.

fever	handy	suitable	furious	fast forward
current	particularly	daily planner	medicine	student union

1. CEOs must use a _____ to make sure they attend all their important meetings.

2. It is important to keep updated on _____ news.

3. Some westerners think that Asians, _____ the Japanese, are incredibly polite.

4. Students can get information at the _____.

5. People often _____ through the previews when they rent a movie.

6. Most parents think that violent movies are not _____ for young children.

7. You should see a doctor if you have a _____ for a long time.

8. _____ should never be shared.

9. Duct tape is so _____. You can use it to fix anything.

10. Parents can become _____ when their children lie.

[02] Independent

Getting Ready to Speak

A. Learn the words.

Key Vocabulary

relationship	significant connection; similarity between two things
worsen	to become or make worse
slim	thin
work out	to exercise
loaded	to be filled with or to contain a lot of

TOEFL® Vocabulary

determining	causing or deciding something
muscular	strong with a good body shape; having a lot of muscles
nutritional	minerals, vitamins, and other healthy things in food
preservatives	things put in food to keep it from rotting or going bad
force	to make someone or something do something using power

B. Read the prompt. Then answer the questions.

Talk about your fast food experience.

1. Where do you usually go when you want to eat fast food?
    I usually go to _____.
2. How often do you eat fast food?
    I eat fast food _____.
3. How do you feel after you eat fast food?
    After eating fast food, I feel _____.

Now practice the questions and answers with a partner.

C. Listen and repeat. Track 1-7

Practice

 A. Read the prompt. Then take turns answering the questions with a partner.

Talk about things that you think make your body healthy and unhealthy.

1. What is one thing you can do to make your body healthier?
2. What is one thing you do that is unhealthy for your body?
3. In terms of your health, what is one thing you want to do to make your body healthier?
4. Do you think you are healthy? Why?

B. With your classmates, make a list of healthy and unhealthy things you can do.

_____

_____

_____

_____

Prompt 2

C. Read the prompt. Then complete the answers with your own information.

What can you do to improve your diet?

What?   I can _____.
How?   I will do this by _____.
When?   I will start doing this _____.
Why?   I want to do this because _____.

Now practice your answers with a partner.

D. Make a list of reasons people do or don't eat fast food with a partner.

_____

_____

_____

_____

E. Read the prompt. Then underline the phrases you could use in your own answer.

> Some people think fast food has made our health worse. What do you think? Why?

Reasons to eat or not eat fast food

- healthy options
- makes us overweight
- lots of fat
- too many preservatives
- easy to get
- convenient

Sample Response and Outline

F. Listen to the sample responses and complete the outlines. `Track 1-8`

Sample response 1

Sample response 2

_____

_____

Reason 1
_____
_____
_____
_____
_____

Reason 2
_____
_____
_____
_____
_____

Reason 1
_____
_____
_____
_____
_____

Reason 2
_____
_____
_____
_____
_____

Conclusion: _____
_____

Conclusion: _____
_____

TOEFL® Vocabulary Practice

G. Fill in the blanks with the correct words.

| determining | muscular | nutritional | preservatives | force |

1. Parents often _____ their children to do things they don't like to do, such as clean their rooms.

2. Professional athletes are almost always more _____ than other people.

3. In philosophy, the thought process is often more important than _____ a correct answer.

4. Food that comes from a bag usually has a lot of _____.

5. All packaged food has its _____ value listed somewhere on the package.

Test

Step 1

Some people think fast food has made our health worse. What do you think? Why?

Step 2

Create an outline for your response.

_____

Reason 1

_____
_____
_____
_____

Reason 2

_____
_____
_____
_____

Conclusion: _____
_____

Step 3

Write a response using your outline from above.

I think that fast food _____.
I think this because _____
_____
_____.
In addition, fast food _____
_____
_____.
Eating fast food _____.

Extension

Work with a partner. Take turns saying your response. Then change partners two more times. Time yourselves!

Your time: _____ seconds   Partner one's time: _____ seconds
Your time: _____ seconds   Partner two's time: _____ seconds
Your time: _____ seconds   Partner three's time: _____ seconds

Integrated

Getting Ready to Speak

A. Learn the words.

Key Vocabulary

marble	a type of hard rock
bronze	a metal made from copper and tin
sculpt	to carve, model, or cast something into a new shape
skilled	able to do something especially well
honor	to show respect to

TOEFL® Vocabulary

intricate	having many parts that are artfully put together
ornate	excessively decorated
dominate	to control or to have much more power
renowned	well known or famous
preserve	to make sure something lasts

B. Read the passage. Then answer the questions.

Roman Sculptures

Roman sculptures were heavily influenced by Greek sculptures. Greek and Roman sculptures were both beautiful and very intricate. They had small elaborate carvings and were very ornate. Sculptures were made to show the greatness of a man or an event. They were often put in public places for all to see.

Roman sculptures were often made from marble or bronze. Romans preferred bronze to marble. Sculptures were often sculpted into the design of buildings, but the most famous sculptures from this period were almost all statues.

1. What were Roman and Greek sculptures made from?
   Roman and Greek sculptures were made from _____ and _____.
2. Why were sculptures made?
   Sculptures were made _____.
3. What do you think this lecture will be about?
   I think this lecture will be about _____.

Now practice the questions and answers with a partner.

C. Listen and repeat. Track 1-9

Practice

A. Read the passage again and underline the key information.

> ### Roman Sculptures
>
> Roman sculptures were heavily influenced by Greek sculptures. Greek and Roman sculptures were both beautiful and very intricate. They had small elaborate carvings and were very ornate. Sculptures were made to show the greatness of a man or an event. They were often put in public places for all to see.
>
> Roman sculptures were often made from marble or bronze. Romans preferred bronze to marble. Sculptures were often sculpted into the design of buildings, but the most famous sculptures from this period were almost all statues.

Note-taking

B. Listen to the lecture and take notes. Track 1-10

Beauty

- Greek and Roman sculptures _____
- People travel to see _____

Style

- Greek and Roman sculptures are _____
- This is because _____

Reasons they were made

- Made to tell _____
- Statues were made to _____

Materials

- Made from _____
- Romans preferred _____

Prompt

C. Read the prompt.

> The professor and the passage give details about sculptures. Why do you think sculptures were so popular in ancient Greece and Rome?

D. Listen to the sample response and complete the outline. Track 1·11

The lecture and passage were about _____.

A. Sculptures

    1. They are _____

    2. They are very _____

B. How it was learned

    1. Greeks _____

    2. Romans _____

C. Uses

    1. Stories _____

    2. Statues _____

D. Materials

    1. Bronze _____

    2. Marble _____

Conclusion: Greek and Roman sculptures are _____.

Speaking Practice

E. Now work with a partner. Take turns saying your own response using the outline from above.

Your time: _____ seconds   Your partner's time: _____ seconds

TOEFL® Vocabulary Practice

F. Fill in the blanks with the correct words.

intricate	ornate	dominates	renowned	preserve

1. Microsoft Windows _____ the world market for computer operating systems.

2. Pavarotti was a world _____ opera singer.

3. A watch is a very _____ device with hundreds of different pieces.

4. Some museums _____ old dinosaur bones.

5. The paintings on the roof of the Sistine Chapel are really _____.

Test

Step 1

Read the passage.

> **Sculpting Bronze and Marble**
>
> Sculpting bronze and marble can be very different. Each requires different materials and different skills. Both bronze and marble can be used to sculpt intricate, ornate patterns, but they are different in how the patterns are achieved. Bronze is stronger so it allows the sculptor to create different shapes and poses. Marble and clay are easily broken. A great example is the famous *Venus Di Milo*. That statue's arms broke off. Bronze was also much more valuable than marble. This is because bronze was used in sculptures, swords, knives, and arrows.

Step 2

Listen to the lecture and take notes. `Track 1-12`

Bronze

- Bronze is an important _____
- It is a combination of _____
- Bronze is both _____
- It was used in both _____
- During wars _____

Marble

- Marble is _____
- A thin piece can _____
- A good example of this is _____
- Feet and legs are _____
- Marble is taken _____

Step 3

Read the prompt.

> The professor and the passage talk about marble and bronze statues. Explain why bronze and marble are good for statues.

Step 4

Create an outline for your response.

The passage and lecture were about _____
_____.

A. Bronze
    1. It is good for _____
    2. It is very _____
    3. During wars _____
    4. There aren't many bronze statues because _____
    _____

B. Marble
    1. Marble is _____
    2. The problem with marble is _____
    3. Examples of problems with marble are _____
    _____
    4. Marble statues often have _____

Step 5

Write a response using your outline from above.

> The passage and lecture were about _____.
> Bronze is good for _____.
> It is good because _____.
> During wars, _____
> _____.
> Marble is _____
> _____.
> The problem with it is that it _____.
> Examples of marble breaking are _____
> _____.
> Marble statues often have thicker _____
> _____.

👥 **Work with a partner. Take turns saying your response. Then change partners two more times. Time yourselves!**

Your time: _____ seconds		Partner one's time: _____ seconds
Your time: _____ seconds		Partner two's time: _____ seconds
Your time: _____ seconds		Partner three's time: _____ seconds

Check-up

Fill in the blanks with the correct words.

| relationship | bronze | slim | work out | sculpt |
| skilled | honor | worsen | marble | loaded |

1. The moon and the ocean have an important _____. The moon causes waves.

2. The Pulitzer Prize is given to _____ the best writing of the year.

3. Fashion models are always _____.

4. Finishing third at the Olympics earns you a(n) _____ medal.

5. It's important to get rest when you're sick so that your health doesn't _____.

6. Christmas stockings are often _____ with small presents for kids.

7. Students learn to draw, paint, and _____ in art class.

8. Genghis Khan and his Mongol army were very _____ horse riders.

9. Fitness trainers say to _____ for at least twenty minutes three times a week.

10. Many important monuments in Europe and America are made of white _____.

Getting Ready to Speak

A. Learn the words.

Key Vocabulary

lead	to guide
miserable	very unhappy
gloomy	having a very sad feeling for a long period of time
dissatisfied	not satisfied or pleased
rural	to do with areas outside a city

TOEFL® Vocabulary

energetic	having a lot of energy
imperative	very important or necessary
captivate	to attract or hold someone's attention
cosmopolitan	knowledgeable and refined; having a worldwide view
ideal	perfect

B. Read the prompt. Then answer the questions.

Talk about the last decision that you made.

1. What did you have to decide?
   I had to decide_____.

2. Were you happy with your decision? Why?
   I was/wasn't happy with my decision because _____.

3. Do you feel that this was an important decision?
   I feel that _____.

Now practice the questions and answers with a partner.

C. Listen and repeat. Track 1-13

Practice

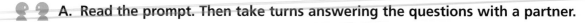

Prompt 1

A. Read the prompt. Then take turns answering the questions with a partner.

Talk about important decisions that you will have to make in the future.

1. What is an important decision that you will have to make in the next five years?
2. Why is this decision important to you?
3. What is an important decision that you have to make in the next ten to fifteen years?
4. Why is this decision important to you?

B. With your classmates, make a list of important decisions you will have to make in the future.

_____

_____

_____

_____

Prompt 2

C. Read the prompt. Then complete the answers with your own information.

Talk about the consequences of the last big decision that you made.

What?	I had to decide _____.
When?	This happened _____.
What happened?	The result of the decision was that _____.
Why?	I decided this because _____.

Now practice your answers with a partner.

D. With a partner, make a list of reasons to take a job.

_____

_____

_____

_____

E. Read the prompt. Then underline the phrases you could use in your own answer.

> What do you think is the most important decision in life? Include specific reasons and details in your explanation.

Reasons to make this decision

- job
- where to live
- spouse
- university
- money
- friends

Sample Response and Outline

F. Listen to the sample responses and complete the outlines. Track 1-14

Sample response 1

Reason 1
_____
_____
_____
_____
_____

Reason 2
_____
_____
_____
_____
_____

Conclusion: _____
_____

Sample response 2

Reason 1
_____
_____
_____
_____
_____

Reason 2
_____
_____
_____
_____
_____

Conclusion: _____
_____

TOEFL® Vocabulary Practice

G. Fill in the blanks with the correct words.

| energetic | imperative | captivates | cosmopolitan | ideal |

1. People from small towns living in big cities often find it hard to adjust to _____ lifestyles.

2. Many people thought that Princess Diana would be a(n) _____ queen.

3. J.K. Rowling's *Harry Potter* series almost always _____ the reader.

4. It is _____ to take a safety course before going scuba diving; otherwise, you can get really hurt.

5. Young children are so _____ that it often makes their mothers tired.

Test

Step 1

Read the prompt.

> What do you think is the most important decision in life? Please include specific reasons and details in your explanation.

Step 2

Create an outline for your response.

```
          _____
```

Reason 1

_____
_____
_____
_____

Reason 2

_____
_____
_____
_____

Conclusion: _____
_____

Step 3

Write a response using your outline from above.

The most important decision that we have to make is _____
_____.

This is so important because _____
_____
_____.

It is also important to _____
_____
_____.

Choosing the right _____ is the most important decision that we have to make.

Extension

**Work with a partner. Take turns saying your response. Then change partners
two more times. Time yourselves!**

Your time: _____ seconds	Partner one's time: _____ seconds
Your time: _____ seconds	Partner two's time: _____ seconds
Your time: _____ seconds	Partner three's time: _____ seconds

Integrated

Getting Ready to Speak

A. Learn the words.

stressed	under emotional pressure
disorder	an illness that prevents part of your body from working properly
unconscious	unable to see, move, feel or be aware of your surroundings
exert	to push or force oneself to do something
deferral	putting something off until a later time

postpone	to change an event to a later time or date
bond	to develop a special relationship with someone
institute	an organization that has a special purpose such as education
grant	to give someone something they have asked for or deserve
deny	to refuse something or say that it is not true

B. Listen to the conversation. Then answer the questions. Track 1-15

1. What are the students discussing?

   The students are discussing _____.

2. What reasons does the student give for postponing the exam?

   Her grandmother _____.

3. What do you think the rest of the conversation will be about?

   I think the rest of the conversation will be about _____.

4. What do you think the student should do?

   I think the student should _____.

Now practice the questions and answers with a partner.

C. Listen and repeat. Track 1-16

Practice

A. **Listen to the full conversation and take notes.** `Track 1-17`

Woman	Man
• Grandmother _____ _____	• Thinks _____
• Doesn't know _____ _____	• Won't grandmother _____ and _____
• Has _____ _____	• Maybe _____ _____
• Studying _____ _____	• Shouldn't exert _____ _____
• Has _____ _____	• Asks if she is _____ _____
• Took care _____ _____	• Seems _____ _____
• Already studied _____ _____	• Can't _____ _____
• Said _____	
• Hard _____	

B. **Use your notes to complete the answers.**

1. What are some reasons the students discuss for not taking the exam?

   The students discuss _____
   _____.

2. What are some reasons the student discusses for taking the exam?

   The student's reasons _____
   _____.

 **Now practice the questions and answers with a partner.**

C. **Read the prompt.**

> The students discuss the reasons for deferring the exam and the reasons for taking it. Describe the reasons for each choice. Then state which choice you think is the better option.

D. Listen to the sample response and complete the outline. `Track 1-18`

The conversation is about _____.

A. Reasons for postponing the exam

   1. Grandmother needs _____

   2. Too distracted _____

   3. Will be easy _____

B. Reasons for taking the exam now

   1. Has studied _____

   2. Grandmother will be _____

   3. Postponing the exam _____

Conclusion: I think _____
_____.

E. Write your own conclusion using the outline from above.

Conclusion: I think _____

because _____.

F. Now work with a partner. Take turns saying your own response using the outline from above.

Your time: _____ seconds   Your partner's time: _____ seconds

G. Fill in the blanks with the correct words.

bond	institute	grant	postpone	deny

1. Universities often _____ scholarships to students who perform well in a particular area.

2. It takes time for a mother to form a(n) _____ with her new baby.

3. California has the top _____ for technology in America.

4. It is impossible to _____ that global warming is becoming a serious problem.

5. If there is too much rain during a baseball game, they often _____ it.

Test

Step 1

Listen to the conversation and take notes. Track 1-19

Woman	Man
• Has a _____ _____	• Should postpone _____ _____
• Requested a _____ _____	• Medicine will _____ _____
• Exerts _____ _____	_____
• Collapsed _____ _____ _____	• Let the _____ _____
• Always had _____ _____	
• Hopes the _____ _____	

Step 2

Read the prompt.

> The students are discussing if the woman should postpone her exams or take them now. Describe the reasons for and against a deferral. What do you think she should do? Why?

Step 3

Create an outline for your response.

The conversation is about _____.

A. Reasons for deferral

    1. Student _____

    2. Medicine _____

    3. Break from _____

B. She collapsed _____

C. Should do the exam now because

    1. she always had _____

    2. she has studied _____

    3. maybe _____

Conclusion: I _____.

Step 4

Write a response using your outline.

The conversation is about _____.
The student _____
_____.
If she defers, _____
_____
_____.
She is not sure what to do because _____
_____
_____.
I would _____
_____
_____.

Extension

Work with a partner. Take turns saying your response. Then change partners
two more times. Time yourselves!

Your time: _____ seconds   Partner one's time: _____ seconds
Your time: _____ seconds   Partner two's time: _____ seconds
Your time: _____ seconds   Partner three's time: _____ seconds

Check-up

Fill in the blanks with the correct words.

stressed	exert	leads	unconscious	deferral
miserable	gloomy	dissatisfied	rural	disorder

1. It is common for students to request a(n) _____ of university admission so they can save some money for their courses.

2. Being a good student in high school and college usually _____ to success later in life.

3. Students often become _____ before big exams.

4. Generally, schools in _____ areas are not as good as ones in the city.

5. A mental _____ can be very difficult to deal with.

6. One symptom of a brain injury is to be _____ for any length of time.

7. Most people feel _____ when they are sick at home with the flu.

8. If you _____ yourself too much during exercise, you may cause damage to your body.

9. In America, if you are _____ with your server at a restaurant, you can choose not to leave a tip.

10. Rainy, cloudy weather often makes people feel _____.

[04] Independent

Getting Ready to Speak

A. Learn the words.

Key Vocabulary

succeed	to prosper or to gain power
hand-in-hand	going together
matters	things or issues that are connected to a subject
failure	lack of success
burst	to explode

TOEFL® Vocabulary

knowledge	information in the mind; specific information
rigors	very severe or very harsh conditions
trying	difficult
necessarily	always or in every case
extraordinarily	beyond what is usual, regular, or ordinary

B. Read the prompt. Then answer the questions.

Talk about something you have a lot of knowledge of.

1. What do you have a lot of knowledge of?
   I have a lot of knowledge _____.

2. How did you get this knowledge?
   I got this knowledge by _____.

3. How will you continue to learn about this?
   I will continue to learn about this by _____.

Now practice the questions and answers with a partner.

C. Listen and repeat. Track 1-20

Practice

A. **Read the prompt. Then take turns answering the questions with a partner.**

> Talk about something that you have done for a long time.

1. What are you experienced at?
2. How long have you been doing this?
3. What have you learned from doing this?
4. How has your experience from doing this changed the way that you do it now?

B. **Make a list of things that you are experienced at with your classmates.**

_____

_____

_____

_____

Prompt 2

C. **Read the prompt. Then complete the answers with your own information.**

> Talk about something that you are good at doing.

What?   I am good at _____.

How?   I became good by _____.

Why?   I am good at this because _____.

How?   I will continue to improve by _____.

Now practice your answers with a partner.

D. **Make a list of words and phrases to describe knowledge and experience with a partner.**

_____

_____

_____

_____

E. Read the prompt. Then underline the phrases you could use in your own response.

> Some people think experience is more important than knowledge. What do you think? Why?

Reasons experience or knowledge is more important

- changing situations
- easier to have failure
- things more difficult than planned
- don't know what may happen
- easier to get
- more trying

Sample Response and Outline

F. Listen to the sample responses and complete the outlines. Track 1-21

Sample response 1		Sample response 2	
⟨_____⟩		⟨_____⟩	
Reasons	**Examples**	**Reasons**	**Examples**
_____	_____	_____	_____
_____	_____	_____	_____
_____	_____	_____	_____
_____	_____	_____	_____
_____	_____	_____	_____

Conclusion: _____

Conclusion: _____

TOEFL® Vocabulary Practice

G. Fill in the blanks with the correct words.

knowledge	rigors	trying	necessarily	extraordinarily

1. The _____ of traveling around the world have largely been eliminated by fast, clean airplanes.

2. Having a sick family member is _____ for the entire family.

3. Some people say _____ is power.

4. George Gershwin was a(n) _____ talented composer at a very young age.

5. A good English reading test score doesn't _____ mean someone can speak English well.

Test

Step 1

Read the prompt.

Some people think experience is more important than knowledge. What do you think? Why?

Step 2

Create an outline for your response.

_____

Reasons
_____
_____
_____
_____

Examples
_____
_____
_____
_____
_____

Conclusion: _____
_____

Step 3

Write a response using your outline from above.

I think that _____.
I think this because _____
_____
_____.
An example of this is _____
_____
_____.
_____ is far more important than _____.

Extension

Work with a partner. Take turns saying your response. Then change partners two more times. Time yourselves!

Your time: _____ seconds   Partner one's time: _____ seconds
Your time: _____ seconds   Partner two's time: _____ seconds
Your time: _____ seconds   Partner three's time: _____ seconds

Integrated

Getting Ready to Speak

A. Learn the words.

organ	a part of the body that performs a special task
nerve	a body part that controls movement and sends and receives messages from the brain
cell	the smallest part of a living thing
neurons	cells of the nervous system that allow different parts of the body to communicate
brain stem	the part of the brain that is closest to the spinal cord

connection	a place where things are joined together
reflex	a sudden physical reaction that you have without thinking about it
functioning	working in the correct way
harmony	a situation where things work together smoothly
maturing	behaving in a reasonable way like an adult

B. Listen to the first part of a lecture. Then answer the questions. Track 1-22

1. What is the lecture mainly about?
   The lecture is about _____.

2. What does the brain produce?
   The brain produces _____.

3. What else do you think the professor will talk about?
   I think the professor _____.

Now practice the questions and answers with a partner.

C. Listen and repeat. Track 1-23

Practice

A. **Listen to the full lecture and take notes.** `Track 1-24`

- The brain produces _____
- Brains form _____
- Patterns change and _____
- Human brain _____
- The first _____
- Controls _____
- The second _____
- Allows us _____
- The third _____
- Second and third _____

B. **Use your notes to complete the answers.**

1. How many sections of the brain does the professor talk about?

   The professor talks about _____

   _____.

2. Which parts of the brain does the professor say must work together? Why?

   The professor says _____

   _____ adulthood.

Now practice the questions and answers with a partner.

C. **Read the prompt.**

> The professor talked about the three main sections of the brain. Using points and examples from the lecture talk about what each part is responsible for.

D. Listen to the sample response and complete the outline. Track 1-25

The lecture is about _____.

A. The brain

    1. Produces _____

    2. Forms _____

    3. Connections _____

B. The human brain _____

    1. Brain stem _____

    2. Mid-brain _____

    3. Neocortex _____

Conclusion: The brain _____.

Speaking Practice

E. Now work with a partner. Take turns saying your own response using the outline from above.

Your time: _____ seconds   Your partner's time: _____ seconds

TOEFL® Vocabulary Practice

F. Fill in the blanks with the correct words.

functioning	maturing	connection	reflexes	harmony

1. Baseball players have excellent _____.

2. The electricity will fail to work if there is a loose _____.

3. Doctors perform surgery if the kidneys stop _____.

4. _____ in the body can be achieved through yoga.

5. Adolescence is an important stage in life before _____ into an adult.

Test

Step 1

Listen to the lecture and take notes. `Track 1-26`

- Concussions are _____
- They are _____
- Brain injury _____
- Symptoms include _____
- Sometimes, _____
- Recovery _____
- Diagnosing _____
- Doctor _____
- If serious, _____

Step 2

Read the prompt.

> The professor describes the causes and symptoms of concussions. Using points and examples from the lecture, describe the causes and symptoms of a concussion.

Step 3

Create an outline for your response.

The lecture is about concussions.

A. Least serious brain injury

   1. Brain is made up of _____

   2. Brain receives _____

B. Causes and symptoms

   1. Commonly _____

   2. Symptoms _____

   _____

C. Doctors _____

D. Recovery _____

Conclusion: Concussions are the least serious head injury but symptoms are not always obvious.

Step 4

Write a response using your outline.

The lecture is about _____. Concussions are very common
and are the _____. The brain
is made up of _____
_____
_____.
Concussions occur _____
_____
_____.
Concussions are diagnosed _____.
They are very easy to diagnose. The recovery _____.
They are the _____.

**Work with a partner. Take turns saying your response. Then change partners
two more times. Time yourselves!**

Your time: _____ seconds   Partner one's time: _____ seconds
Your time: _____ seconds   Partner two's time: _____ seconds
Your time: _____ seconds   Partner three's time: _____ seconds

Check-up

Fill in the blanks with the correct words.

organ	succeed	neurons	matters	hand-in-hand
failure	nerve	cells	brain stem	bursting

1. _____ donors can save or improve the quality of someone else's life.

2. The American CIA's Bay of Pigs invasion of Cuba was a complete disaster and a total _____.

3. The optic _____ connects the eye to the brain.

4. Children often ask their parents for advice on important _____.

5. _____ typically receive and carry nerve impulses away from the cell body.

6. All information to and from our body passes through the _____ on the way to or from the brain.

7. A good orange is _____ with juice when you bite into it.

8. Red blood _____ transport oxygen and carbon dioxide throughout the body.

9. A good job and family often go _____ with a happy life.

10. People who often _____ are also usually very competitive.

[05] Independent

Getting Ready to Speak

A. Learn the words.

Key Vocabulary

special effects	images created with special technical skills
explosion	a violent expansion or bursting with a loud noise
come to life	to appear life-like; to become animated
nursing home	place where elderly people live and are cared for
discuss	to talk about something

TOEFL® Vocabulary

innovative	new and creative
incredible	almost impossible; amazing
compliment	to praise
visit	to spend time with someone or something
article	a piece of writing that forms part of a publication, such as a newspaper

B. Read the prompt. Then answer the questions.

> Talk about your hobbies and things that you like to do.

1. What is your hobby?
My hobby is _____.

2. How much time do you spend enjoying your hobby?
I spend _____.

3. Where do you do your hobby?
I do my hobby _____.

 **Now practice the questions and answers with a partner.**

C. Listen and repeat. `Track 1-27`

Practice

Prompt 1

A. **Read the prompt. Then take turns answering the questions with a partner.**

Talk about a place in your city that you like to go to.

1. Where do you like to go?
2. Why do you like going there?
3. How often do you go?
4. Do you wish you could go more often? Why?

B. **With your classmates, make a list of places that you like to go to.**

_____

_____

_____

_____

Prompt 2

C. **Read the prompt. Then complete the answers with your own information.**

Talk about a place that you have to go to but do not really like going to.

Where?   I have to go to _____.

How often? I go there _____.

What?   When I'm there, I have to _____.

Why?   I have to go to _____

            because _____.

Now practice your answers with a partner.

D. **Make a list of things that you spend a lot of time doing with a partner.**

_____

_____

_____

_____

E. Read the prompt. Then underline the phrases you could use in your own response.

> Where do you often go, and why do you go there? Include specific reasons and details in your explanation.

Reasons you often go somewhere

- to have fun
- to learn something new
- to get innovative ideas
- to make my mom happy
- to hang out
- to help myself

Sample Response and Outline

F. Listen to the sample responses and complete the outlines. `Track 1-28`

Sample response 1   **Sample response 2**

_____   _____

Reason 1   **Reason 2**   **Reason 1**   **Reason 2**

_____   _____   _____   _____
_____   _____   _____   _____
_____   _____   _____   _____
_____   _____   _____   _____
_____   _____   _____   _____

Conclusion: _____   **Conclusion:** _____
_____   _____

TOEFL® Vocabulary Practice

G. Fill in the blanks with the correct words.

innovative	incredible	compliment	visit	articles

1. Teachers often _____ their students when they do well in class.
2. The most important stories in the news are usually _____ on the front page of the newspaper.
3. Many tourists in Italy cannot believe how _____ Italian food is.
4. Apple is one of the most _____ companies in the world.
5. In 1972, Richard Nixon became the first American President to _____ with Mao Zedong.

Test

Step 1

Read the prompt.

Where do you often go, and why do you go there? Include specific reasons and details in your explanation.

Step 2

Create an outline for your response.

⬭ _____

Reason 1

_____
_____
_____
_____

Reason 2

_____
_____
_____
_____

Conclusion: _____

_____

Step 3

Write a response using your outline from above.

I often go to _____.
I go there because _____
_____
_____.
Another reason I go there is because _____
_____
_____.
I spend a lot of time at _____.

👤👤 **Work with a partner. Take turns saying your response. Then change partners two more times. Time yourselves!**

Your time: _____ seconds   Partner one's time: _____ seconds
Your time: _____ seconds   Partner two's time: _____ seconds
Your time: _____ seconds   Partner three's time: _____ seconds

Integrated

Getting Ready to Speak

A. Learn the words.

Key Vocabulary

advise	to give someone advice or ideas on how to solve his or her problem
reform	a change
peacefully	in a quiet or calm way
victim	a person or thing that suffers because of something or someone
optimistic	thinking in a happy or positive way

TOEFL® Vocabulary

enable	to help or assist
pros and cons	advantages and disadvantages
stable	regular; unchanging
flexibility	ability to move or change
rigid	solid or unchanging

B. Read the announcement. Then answer the questions.

> **New Dorm "Quiet Hours"**
>
> All dorm residents please be advised that the "quiet hours" for this building are being reformed. Currently, the quiet hours are from 11:00 p.m. until 5:00 a.m. We have recently received many letters from residents stating that they are unhappy with such short "quiet hours." As a result, the new hours will be from 10:00 p.m. until 6:00 a.m. Please do not play loud music, have loud parties, or make other noise between these hours. This will enable all residents to live peacefully in our building.

1. What will happen?
The dorm will _____.

2. Why is the dorm doing this?
They are changing the hours because _____
_____.

3. What do you think the conversation will be about?
I think the conversation will be about _____.

Now practice the questions and answers with a partner.

C. Listen and repeat. `Track 1-29`

Practice

A. Read the announcement again and underline key information.

> ### New Dorm "Quiet Hours"
>
> All dorm residents please be advised that the "quiet hours" for this building are being reformed. Currently, the quiet hours are from 11:00 p.m. until 5:00 a.m. We have recently received many letters from residents stating that they are unhappy with such short "quiet hours." As a result, the new hours will be from 10:00 p.m. until 6:00 a.m. Please do not play loud music, have loud parties, or make other noise between these hours. This will enable all residents to live peacefully in our building.

Note-taking

B. Listen to the conversation and take notes. `Track 1-30`

Man	Woman
• Is having _____ • Didn't know _____ _____ • Thinks it will _____ _____ • Thinks they should be _____ _____	• Can't _____ • Has a _____ • Thinks there are _____ _____ • Is _____ • Has trouble _____ _____ • Other students have _____ _____ • Likes _____ _____ • People need to be _____ _____ and _____

Prompt

C. Read the prompt.

> The woman expresses her opinion about the dorm changing its "quiet hours." State her opinion and explain the reasons she gives for holding this opinion.

D. Listen to the sample response and complete the outline. [Track 1-31]

The woman is _____.

A. The woman

    1. thinks _____

    2. thinks it will enable _____

    3. has _____

B. She likes _____

C. Students

    1. have _____

      • The woman is happy that _____

    2. can still have _____

      • Be _____

      • Be _____

Speaking Practice

E. Now work with a partner. Take turns saying your own response using the outline from above.

Your time: _____ seconds   Your partner's time: _____ seconds

TOEFL® Vocabulary Practice

F. Fill in the blanks with the correct words.

enable	flexibility	pros and cons	rigid	stable

1. There are many _____ to studying English abroad.

2. Good English skills will _____ you to get a better job.

3. _____ is an asset in the workplace.

4. Some parents are very _____ about rules.

5. It's important to have a(n) _____ job.

Test

Step 1

Read the announcement.

> **Changes in the Dorm Guest Policy**
>
> All Dorm Residents:
> Beginning March 1st there will be some changes to the dorm guest policy. There have been too many outsiders spending time in the dorms. We have been advised that some of these people have been the cause of excessive noise at late hours of the day. The new "guest hours," posted below are intended to make dorm life more stable. These hours may seem very rigid, but no exceptions will be made. Security will be patrolling the building outside of these hours. This will enable all residents to study and live peacefully.

Step 2

Listen to the conversation and take notes. Track 1-32

Woman	Man
• Have been _____	• Thinks _____
• Guests will _____ _____	• Had problems with _____
• Some students will _____ _____	• It's hard _____ _____
• Thinks it will _____ _____	• Is _____
• There will be _____	• People will _____
• Everyone _____ _____	• Will bring _____
	• The majority _____ _____

Step 3

Read the prompt.

> The man expresses his opinion about the dorm guest hours changing. State his opinion, and explain the reasons he has for holding that opinion.

Step 4

Create an outline for your response.

The man thinks _____.

A. It gets really _____

B. He

    1. thinks it's hard _____

    2. has had problems with _____

    3. is happy _____

C. People

    1. are going to _____

    2. will have fewer _____

    3. will be _____

D. The building will be _____

Step 5

Write a response using your outline from above.

> The man thinks _____. At the moment
> it gets _____, and he thinks it's hard to
> _____
> _____.
> Therefore, he is happy _____.
> He also thinks that people are going to _____
> _____
> _____
> _____.

Work with a partner. Take turns saying your response. Then change partners two more times. Time yourselves!

Your time: _____ seconds   Partner one's time: _____ seconds

Your time: _____ seconds   Partner two's time: _____ seconds

Your time: _____ seconds   Partner three's time: _____ seconds

Check-up

Fill in the blanks with the correct words.

advise	special effects	explosion	come to life	nursing home
discuss	optimistic	peacefully	reformed	victims

1. *Star Wars* had very original _____.
2. Hostages are innocent _____ of terrorism.
3. When people get older and can't take care of themselves, they often move to a(n) _____.
4. Education systems are often _____ according to new philosophies.
5. Elderly people often enjoy living _____ in the countryside.
6. Parents often _____ their children when they have problems.
7. The voices in *Shrek* help to make the characters _____.
8. You must not smoke at a gas station so that you don't cause a(n) _____.
9. It's better to be _____ than pessimistic.
10. Professors in universities often ask students to _____ current events.

[06] Independent

Getting Ready to Speak

A. Learn the words.

Key Vocabulary	
operate	to function; to make something work
employee	a paid worker
bargain	a cheap purchase or price
deal	a beneficial business agreement or transaction
pocket	a small pouch on clothes to put things in

TOEFL® Vocabulary	
local	a person who lives in a nearby area
standard of living	level of material comfort that someone has
chain store	a store that is the same in many locations
hard-earned	something obtained through a lot of difficult work
wisely	showing good sense

B. Read the prompt. Then answer the questions.

> Talk about where you often go shopping.

1. What is the name of the store where you most often go shopping.

    I go shopping most often at _____.

2. Why do you go shopping there?

    I go shopping there because _____.

3. Do you prefer shopping at large stores or small stores? Why?

    I prefer shopping at _____ because _____.

Now practice the questions and answers with a partner.

C. Listen and repeat. `Track 1-33`

Practice

Prompt 1

 A. Read the prompt. Then take turns answering the questions with a partner.

> Talk about your favorite chain restaurant.

1. What is your favorite chain restaurant?
2. Why is it your favorite chain restaurant?
3. What is your favorite item at the restaurant?
4. Do you prefer this restaurant to similar independent restaurants? Why?

B. Make a list of good and bad things about chain stores with your classmates.

_____

_____

_____

_____

Prompt 2

C. Read the prompt. Then complete the answers with your own information.

> Talk about an independent store that you know of.

What?   They sell _____.

Who?   The owners of the store _____.

Why?   I would/wouldn't shop there because _____

_____.

Where?   The store is located _____.

Now tell your answers to a partner.

D. Make a list of words and phrases that describe small stores with a partner.

_____

_____

_____

_____

E. Read the prompt. Then underline the phrases you could use in your own response.

> Some people think it is better to shop at independent stores rather than chain stores. What do you think? Why?

Reasons to shop at independent stores

- better selection
- better service
- cheaper
- support locals
- more convenient
- better quality

Sample Response and Outline

F. Listen to the sample responses and complete the outlines. `Track 1-34`

Sample response 1

Reason 1
_____
_____
_____
_____
_____

Reason 2
_____
_____
_____
_____
_____

Conclusion: _____
_____

Sample response 2

Reason 1
_____
_____
_____
_____
_____

Reason 2
_____
_____
_____
_____
_____

Conclusion: _____
_____

TOEFL® Vocabulary Practice

G. Fill in the blanks with the correct words.

| locals | standard of living | chain stores | hard-earned | wisely |

1. Warren Buffet is famous for _____ investing in companies and making lots of money.
2. People in Africa have a much lower _____ than Europeans have.
3. McDonald's is one of the most popular _____ in the world.
4. When you visit a city, _____ can tell you a lot of information about it.
5. Many people feel better after a _____ accomplishment instead of one that was really easy.

Test

Step 1

Read the prompt.

Some people think it is better to shop at independent stores rather than chain stores. What do you think? Why?

Step 2

Create an outline for your response.

_____

Reason 1

_____

_____

_____

_____

Conclusion: _____

_____

Reason 2

_____

_____

_____

_____

Step 3

Write a response using your outline from above.

I think it is better to shop at _____.

I like to shop at _____ because _____

_____

_____.

They are also better because _____

_____

_____.

It is best to shop at _____.

Extension

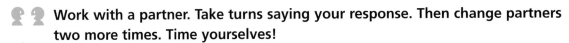 Work with a partner. Take turns saying your response. Then change partners two more times. Time yourselves!

Your time: _____ seconds	Partner one's time: _____ seconds
Your time: _____ seconds	Partner two's time: _____ seconds
Your time: _____ seconds	Partner three's time: _____ seconds

Integrated

Getting Ready to Speak

A. Learn the words.

Key Vocabulary

fortunately	luckily
corrupt	immoral or dishonest
homeland	country where someone is born
intensive	very thorough and in great detail
root for	to support a team or organization

TOEFL® Vocabulary

minority	a small group within a larger group
inherent	the nature of something
currency	money
regime	a system of government
variable	something that is able to change suddenly

B. Read the passage. Then answer the questions.

African Refugees

Many Africans have become refugees. They have had to do so because of fighting in their home country. They often were minorities in their country and had to flee to save their lives. They often move to new places in America and Europe. Their lives at first are very difficult. They face problems that are inherent in moving to a new country. They must learn new languages, a new currency, customs, and an entirely new way of life. Fortunately, foundations are set up to help them adjust to their new lives. It takes time, but eventually they get comfortable in their new homes.

1. Why do refugees flee their homelands?
   They have to flee because _____.
2. What are some problems that refugees face in a new country?
   They face problems with _____.
3. What do you think this lecture will be about?
   I think this lecture will be about _____.

👤👤 **Now practice the questions and answers with a partner.**

🎧 **C. Listen and repeat.** `Track 1-35`

Practice

A. Read the passage again and underline the key information.

> ### African Refugees
>
> Many Africans have become refugees. They have had to do so because of fighting in their home country. They often were minorities in their country and had to flee to save their lives. They often move to new places in America and Europe. Their lives at first are very difficult. They face problems that are inherent in moving to a new country. They must learn new languages, a new currency, customs, and an entirely new way of life. Fortunately, foundations are set up to help them adjust to their new lives. It takes time, but eventually they get comfortable in their new homes.

Note-taking

B. Listen to the lecture and take notes. `Track 1-36`

Leaving

- Their governments _____
- There isn't enough _____
- They are often _____

Problems

- They cannot _____
  - They overcome this by _____
  - They have to _____
- The weather _____

Organizations/other refugees

- They help to _____
- They help adjust _____

In the end

- They learn to _____

Prompt

C. Read the prompt.

The professor and the passage give details about how refugees adjust to life in a new homeland. Explain the different methods that refugees use to adjust.

D. Listen to the sample response and complete the outline. `Track 1-37`

The lecture and the passage were about _____.

A. They leave because

   1. their governments are _____

   2. their homelands don't have _____

   3. they are worried that _____

B. The problems they face are

   1. they often cannot _____

   2. the weather is _____

C. Help

   1. _____ help refugees adjust

   2. They get help _____

   3. They teach them useful things like _____

Speaking Practice

E. Now work with a partner. Take turns saying your own response using the outline from above.

Your time: _____ seconds   Your partner's time: _____ seconds

TOEFL® Vocabulary Practice

F. Fill in the blanks with the correct words.

minority	inherent	currency	regime	variables

1. Ethnic Chinese are a powerful _____ in Singapore.

2. When going to a new country, you have to adjust to using a new _____.

3. When a new president takes office, he or she starts a new _____.

4. There are so many _____ for astronauts on spaceships that they can't possibly be prepared for them all.

5. There is a small but _____ possibility of death when you go scuba diving.

Test

Step 1

Read the passage.

Iraqi Refugees

Since war started in Iraq in 2003, millions of Iraqis had to flee their homeland. Their old corrupt regime was defeated, but intensive fighting continued. Many Iraqis had to flee to save their lives. They had to sell what they could, take what currency they had, and flee to a neighboring country. The Iraqis fortunately brought their old culture and heritage with them to the new country. They brought their food, language, religion, and heritage. They soon started to practice these things in their new home. Sections of large cities, like Damascus, are now called little Baghdad. This is due to the huge impact and number of Iraqis living there.

Step 2

Listen to the lecture and take notes. `Track 1-38`

How it started

- In Iraq, the regime was _____
- Regime was defeated but _____
- This made people _____

Where they went

- They went to _____
- They come with their own _____

What they do

- They make _____
- They start _____
- This is so _____

Theater

- Iraqis have _____
- Plays show _____
- Plays are _____
- Enjoy them because _____

Step 3

Read the prompt.

The professor and the passage talk about Iraqi refugees. Explain why the Iraqis left Iraq and what they do in their new countries.

Step 4

Create an outline for your response.

This passage and lecture were about _____.

A. The Iraqi regime was _____

    1. The regime was defeated but _____

    2. This led to _____

B. Iraqis went to _____

C. They made _____

    1. They started _____

    2. They felt more comfortable because _____

    _____

D. The theater

    1. Iraqis have a long _____

    2. They write _____

    3. The plays are _____

    4. Iraqi people _____

Step 5

Write a response using your outline from above.

>   This passage and lecture were about _____. The Iraqi
> regime _____.
> Iraqis left to _____. They made their lives _____.
> They did this by _____
> _____.
> The plays are _____
> _____.
> Iraqis love the theater because _____
> _____.

Work with a partner. Take turns saying your response. Then change partners two more times. Time yourselves!

Your time: _____ seconds		Partner one's time: _____ seconds	
Your time: _____ seconds		Partner two's time: _____ seconds	
Your time: _____ seconds		Partner three's time: _____ seconds	

Check-up

Fill in the blanks with the correct words.

bargains	fortunately	deal	employees	corrupt
operate	pocket	homeland	intensive	rooting

1. People can lose their money and their keys if there is a hole in their
   _____.

2. People often end up _____ for the same sports team as their father.

3. Older people often find it difficult to _____ new technology.

4. _____ have much less power in a business than the owners.

5. _____ governments rarely look after the well-being of their people.

6. During the opening ceremony at the Olympics, athletes get to carry the flag of their
   _____.

7. Schooling to become a doctor is very _____.

8. It is hard to find good _____ at expensive department stores.

9. When things are on sale, you can usually get a good _____.

10. In 1981, someone tried to shoot President Reagan. _____, the President
    was OK.

[Review 1]

Step 1

Read the prompt.

Describe your relative that is the most fun.

Step 2

Create an outline for your response.

_____

Reason 1

_____
_____
_____
_____

Reason 2

_____
_____
_____
_____

Conclusion: _____
_____

Step 3

Write a response using your outline from above.

My favorite relative is my _____. I like being with _____
because _____.
For example, _____.
My _____ is also great because _____
_____.
When I am with _____ we always _____.
My _____ is the most fun because _____
_____.

👤👤 **Work with a partner. Take turns saying your response. Then change partners two more times. Time yourselves!**

Your time: _____ seconds   Partner one's time: _____ seconds
Your time: _____ seconds   Partner two's time: _____ seconds
Your time: _____ seconds   Partner three's time: _____ seconds

Step 1

Read the announcement.

> ### Lowering of the Study Abroad Standards
> The university has decided to lower the grade requirements to study abroad. The university will grant permission to any student who has passing grades in all of his or her classes to study abroad. This will enable more students to take advantage of this program. The university realizes the rigors of college life. Students have many responsibilities. The university is also about experiencing new things. The university feels it does not want to deny the students opportunities to gain knowledge because they do not necessarily have perfect grades.

Step 2

Listen to the conversation and take notes. **Track 1-39**

Man	Woman
• He is very _____	• Thinks there are _____
• He will go to _____	_____
_____	• Should be a _____
• Was worried that _____	_____
_____	• Thinks she is in _____
• Thinks there are only _____	• Thought levels _____
_____	_____
• Going will _____	• Is happy _____
_____	_____
• School shouldn't _____	
_____	

Step 3

Read the prompt.

> The man expresses his opinion on the lowering of the grades needed to study abroad. State his opinion and explain the reasons he gives for holding that opinion.

Step 4

Create an outline for your response.

The conversation is about _____.

A. The man's opinion is that _____

    1. Students gain _____

    2. Thinks there are _____

    3. Schools shouldn't _____

B. He will go to _____

C. He was worried that _____

D. The woman thinks _____

    1. Studying abroad _____

    2. But, she is _____

Step 5

Write a response using your outline from above.

> The conversation is about _____.
> The man thinks that _____
> _____.
> He thinks that _____
> _____. Schools shouldn't _____
> _____. He will go _____.
> He was worried that _____
> _____. The woman thinks _____
> _____. She thinks that _____
> _____.
> But, _____.

Extension

Work with a partner. Take turns saying your response. Then change partners two more times. Time yourselves!

Your time: _____ seconds   Partner one's time: _____ seconds

Your time: _____ seconds   Partner two's time: _____ seconds

Your time: _____ seconds   Partner three's time: _____ seconds

Step 1

Listen to the lecture and take notes. **Track 1-40**

- Teeth and tongue help with _____
- Proper treatment will _____
- Nice smile can _____
- Smile can _____
- The tongue is _____
- Moves around to _____
- Teeth let us make _____
- Both tongue and teeth _____
- Healthy mouth _____
- Should _____

Step 2

Read the prompt.

> The professor describes how our mouth, teeth, and tongue help us to communicate. Using points and examples from the lecture, describe how these things help us to communicate effectively.

Step 3

Create an outline for your response.

This lecture is about how your mouth, tongue, and teeth help you communicate.

A. Smiles
   1. A nice smile can _____
   2. It can also _____
B. The tongue
   1. It is very _____
   2. It moves around to _____
   3. Also it _____
C. Teeth
   1. They help us make _____
   2. Like the tongue, they also _____
D. Mouth
   1. A healthy mouth _____
   2. It is really important to _____
   _____

Step 4

Write a response using your outline.

> This lecture is about _____.
> Your mouth helps you smile. This is important because _____
> _____.
> The tongue _____
> _____
> _____.
> The teeth _____.
> Like the tongue _____.
> A healthy mouth _____.
> It is important to _____.

Work with a partner. Take turns saying your response. Then change partners two more times. Time yourselves!

Your time: _____ seconds   Partner one's time: _____ seconds

Your time: _____ seconds   Partner two's time: _____ seconds

Your time: _____ seconds   Partner three's time: _____ seconds

Step 1

Read the prompt.

Do you think you should do a job for money or for the love of it?

Step 2

Create an outline for your response.

_____

For the love
Pros

_____
_____
_____

Cons

_____
_____

For the money
Pros

_____
_____
_____

Cons

_____
_____

Conclusion: _____
_____

Step 3

Write a response using your outline.

It is important to do a job for _____. This is imperative because _____
_____
In addition, _____
_____. Others say it is better to work for _____.
I disagree. Doing things for _____
_____.
You will _____.
You should do work for _____.

Work with a partner. Take turns saying your response. Then change partners two more times. Time yourselves!

Your time: _____ seconds   Partner one's time: _____ seconds
Your time: _____ seconds   Partner two's time: _____ seconds
Your time: _____ seconds   Partner three's time: _____ seconds

Getting Ready to Speak

A. Learn the words.

Key Vocabulary

mess up	to ruin something; to make something bad
canoeing	traveling by canoe
traffic jam	many cars together on a crowded street that are not moving quickly
rush-hour	the time of day when many people go to and from work
flow	to move freely from one place to another

TOEFL® Vocabulary

modify	to make small changes
official	a person who has an important job or position
resolve	to make a decision; to find a solution to a problem
priority	something given the greatest importance
smooth	steady and uninterrupted

B. Read the prompt. Then answer the questions.

Talk about where you live.

1. Which city do you live in?

   I live in _____.

2. Where is your city?

   My city is located _____.

3. What is your city famous for?

   My city is famous for _____.

👥 **Now practice the questions and answers with a partner.**

🎧 C. **Listen and repeat.** Track 2-1

Practice

A. Read the prompt. Then take turns answering the questions with a partner.

Talk about different aspects of your hometown.

1. How do you feel about your hometown's schools? Why?
2. How do you feel about your hometown's weather? Why?
3. How do you feel about entertainment in your hometown? Why?
4. How do you feel about how your hometown looks? Why?

B. Make a list of things that a city can improve with your classmates.

_____

_____

_____

_____

Prompt 2

C. Read the prompt. Then complete the answers with your own information.

What would you do to improve your hometown?

What?	I would improve the _____.
How?	I would improve the _____ by _____.
Why?	I would improve this because _____.
Where?	I would first start these improvements by _____
	_____.

Now practice your answers with a partner.

D. Make a list of things that are bad about cities with a partner.

_____

_____

_____

_____

E. Read the prompt. Then underline the phrases you could use in your own response.

What do you dislike about your hometown, and why do you dislike it? Include specific reasons and details in your explanation.

Reasons to dislike a city

- ugly scenery
- bad pollution
- not enough parks
- unfriendly people
- too many people
- everyone is in a hurry

Sample Response and Outline

F. Listen to the sample responses and complete the outlines. Track 2-2

Sample response 1		Sample response 2	
Reasons	**Examples**	**Reasons**	**Examples**
_____	_____	_____	_____
_____	_____	_____	_____
_____	_____	_____	_____
_____	_____	_____	_____
_____	_____		

Conclusion: _____

Conclusion: _____

TOEFL® Vocabulary Practice

G. Fill in the blanks with the correct words.

modify   official   resolved   priority   smoother

1. You must be very careful when you try to _____ electronic gadgets. They break easily.
2. Sir Alex Ferguson is the head _____ of Manchester United.
3. Flying in an airplane is _____ than riding a horse.
4. Judges have traditionally _____ arguments and issues between people.
5. John F. Kennedy said that it would be a top _____ for America to put a man on the moon.

Test

Step 1

Read the prompt.

What do you dislike about your hometown, and why do you dislike it? Include specific reasons and details in your explanation.

Step 2

Create an outline for your response.

_____

Reasons

_____
_____
_____
_____
_____

Examples

_____
_____
_____
_____
_____

Conclusion: _____
_____

Step 3

Write a response using your outline from above.

I dislike the _____ of my city. I dislike it
because _____
_____
_____.
For example, _____
_____
_____.
I really wish that _____.

Extension

Work with a partner. Take turns saying your response. Then change partners two more times. Time yourselves!

Your time: _____ seconds

Your time: _____ seconds

Your time: _____ seconds

Partner one's time: _____ seconds

Partner two's time: _____ seconds

Partner three's time: _____ seconds

Integrated

Getting Ready to Speak

A. Learn the words.

Key Vocabulary

distraction	something that changes the focus of your attention
select	to choose
scope	the range of one's perceptions, thoughts, or actions
living standards	the amount of wealth and comfort that someone expects
tremendous	very large in amount or size; wonderful

TOEFL® Vocabulary

estate	a large area of land with property
deviate	to stray away from something
intrinsic	being part of the basic nature or character of someone or something
subordinate	a person in a lower position of power
tension	stress between people, groups, nations, etc.

B. Listen to the first part of a conversation. Then answer the questions. Track 2-3

1. What are the students discussing?

   The students are discussing _____.

2. What reasons does the student give for living at home?

   The student says _____.

3. What do you think the rest of the conversation will be about?

   I think the rest of the conversation will be about _____

   _____.

4. What do you think the student should do?

   I think the student should _____.

Now practice the questions and answers with a partner.

C. Listen and repeat. Track 2-4

Practice

◯ **A. Listen to the full conversation and take notes.** `Track 2-5`

Man	Woman
• Thinking of _____ _____	• More freedom _____
• Parents _____ _____	
• They like that _____ _____	• Says he seems _____ _____
• Doesn't want _____ _____	
• Wants _____ _____	• Thinks it will _____ _____
• Being on campus _____ _____	• He would _____ _____
• Brother treats him _____ _____	• Asks _____
• Causes _____	
• The living standards on campus are _____	

B. Use your notes to complete the answers.

1. What are some reasons the students discuss for buying a car to get to university?

   The students discuss _____

   _____.

2. What are some reasons the students discuss for staying on campus?

   The students discuss _____

   _____.

👤👤 **Now practice the questions and answers with a partner.**

C. Read the prompt.

> The students discuss buying a car to get to university and living on campus. Describe the advantages of both choices. Then state which choice you think is best.

D. Listen to the sample response and complete the outline. `Track 2-6`

The conversation is about _____.

A. Advantages of buying a car

   1. Could live _____

   2. It's intrinsic _____

   3. Will have _____

B. Advantages to staying on campus

   1. Closer to _____

   2. Facilities _____

Conclusion: I think _____

_____.

E. Write your own conclusion using the outline from above.

Conclusion: I think _____

          because _____.

Speaking Practice

F. Now work with a partner. Take turns saying your own response using the outline from above.

Your time: _____ seconds   Your partner's time: _____ seconds

TOEFL® Vocabulary Practice

G. Fill in the blanks with the correct words.

deviate	estates	tension	intrinsic	subordinates

1. A General of an army has many _____.

2. When telling a true story, it is important not to _____ from the truth.

3. Violence is an _____ part of some contact sports.

4. The English countryside used to have many _____.

5. There is a lot of _____ between South and North Korea.

Test

Step 1

Listen to the conversation and take notes. Track 2-7

Woman	Man
• Can't decide _____ _____	• Thinks _____ _____
• Mom is _____ _____ _____	• Campus accommodation _____ _____
• Great experience _____ _____	• All rooms _____ _____
• Tremendous _____ _____	• Doesn't have _____
• Doesn't want _____ _____	• Could use free _____ _____
• Good to get _____	• Make time _____

Step 2

Read the prompt.

> The students are discussing living with parents while at university or living on campus. Describe the advantages and disadvantages of both choices. Then state which option you would take and why.

Step 3

Create an outline for your response.

The conversation is about _____

_____.

A. Advantages and disadvantages to living at home
    1. Would _____
    2. Standard of living _____
    3. Take up _____
B. Living on campus _____
C. Advantages to living on campus
    1. Has _____
    2. Won't _____
    3. Get _____
Conclusion: I would prefer _____

_____

Step 4

Write a response using your outline.

The conversation is about _____.
Living at home _____
_____.
However, living on campus _____.
The university has _____
_____.
I would prefer _____
_____.

Work with a partner. Take turns saying your answer. Then change partners two more times. Time yourselves!

Your time: _____ seconds   Partner one's time: _____ seconds

Your time: _____ seconds   Partner two's time: _____ seconds

Your time: _____ seconds   Partner three's time: _____ seconds

Check-up

Fill in the blanks with the correct words.

distraction	living standards	rush-hour	tremendous	flow
messes up	canoeing	traffic jams	scope	select

1. Somebody who is liberal often has a wider _____ on different issues.

2. _____ is a great way to see nature and get some exercise.

3. _____ are usually bigger problems in big urban cities rather than small rural ones.

4. It is very frustrating when the server at a restaurant _____ your order.

5. It is widely accepted that the _____ in Europe are higher than those in China.

6. A dam is a big wall that stops the _____ of a river.

7. Winning an Olympic gold medal is a _____ accomplishment.

8. In co-ed schools the opposite sex can be a big _____.

9. There are often a lot of radio commercials during _____ because everyone is in their cars.

10. When entering university, students have to _____ what subject they want to study.

[08] Independent

Getting Ready to Speak

A. Learn the words.

Key Vocabulary

precious	valued
errand	a small thing you must do
chore	a small task to be done, often in the home
picky	very choosy
hassle	a difficulty or thing that causes trouble

TOEFL® Vocabulary

thereby	by means of that
intimately	closely; in a personal relationship
involve	to take part
pursuit	a hobby or passion
cater	to provide what is wanted

B. Read the prompt. Then answer the questions.

Talk about your favorite food.

1. What is your favorite food?

   My favorite food is _____.

2. Who makes this food best?

   _____ makes this food best.

3. Why is this food the best?

   _____ is the best because _____

   _____.

Now practice the questions and answers with a partner.

C. Listen and repeat. `Track 2-8`

Practice

👤👤 **A. Read the prompt. Then take turns answering the questions with a partner.**

> **Talk about your mom's cooking.**

1. Do you like your mom's cooking? Why?
2. What does your mom make best?
3. How often do you get to eat your mom's cooking?
4. How much time does your mom spend preparing food?

B. Make a list of words and phrases that describe good food with your classmates.

_____

_____

_____

_____

Prompt 2

C. Read the prompt. Then complete the answers with your own information.

> **Talk about your favorite restaurant.**

Which?	My favorite restaurant is _____.
Where?	The restaurant is located _____.
What?	They make _____.
Why?	I like this restaurant because _____
	_____.

👤👤 **Now practice your answers with a partner.**

D. Make a list of things that are difficult about cooking with a partner.

_____

_____

_____

_____

E. Read the prompt. Then underline the phrases you could use in your own response.

> Some people think it is better to eat at home than in a restaurant. What do you think? Why?

Reasons to eat at home or at a restaurant

- better food
- less time
- healthier
- cheaper
- less hassle
- faster

Sample Response and Outline

F. Listen to the sample responses and complete the outlines. `Track 2-9`

Sample response 1	Sample response 2

Sample response 1

⟨ _____ ⟩

Reason 1	Reason 2
_____	_____
_____	_____
_____	_____
_____	_____
_____	_____

Conclusion: _____
_____

Sample response 2

⟨ _____ ⟩

Reason 1	Reason 2
_____	_____
_____	_____
_____	_____
_____	_____
_____	_____

Conclusion: _____
_____

TOEFL® Vocabulary Practice

G. Fill in the blanks with the correct words.

thereby	intimately	involved	pursuit	cater

1. Restaurants and hotels often _____ specifically for movie stars and important people.
2. Much of the world was _____ in World War II.
3. Best friends are often _____ involved in their friends' lives.
4. Watching English TV will improve your vocabulary, _____ increasing your overall ability.
5. A good university is often an important _____ of high school students.

Test

Step 1

Read the prompt.

Some people think it is better to eat at home than in a restaurant. What do you think? Why?

Step 2

Create an outline for your response.

```
        _____
```

Reason 1

_____
_____
_____
_____

Reason 2

_____
_____
_____
_____

Conclusion: _____
_____

Step 3

Write a response using your outline from above.

It is better to eat _____.
This is because _____
_____
_____.
Eating at _____ is also great because _____
_____
_____.
I will always _____.

Work with a partner. Take turns saying your response. Then change partners two more times. Time yourselves!

Your time: _____ seconds   Partner one's time: _____ seconds
Your time: _____ seconds   Partner two's time: _____ seconds
Your time: _____ seconds   Partner three's time: _____ seconds

Integrated

Getting Ready to Speak

A. Learn the words.

snorkel	a tube that allows a swimmer to breathe while their face is under water
coral	plant-like sea creatures with hard colored skeletons living in warm sea water
bleaching	making something white or colorless
algae	a simple plant without stems or leaves that lives in or near water
marine	relating to the sea

exquisite	beautiful
prompt	to initiate
prediction	a statement guessing that something will happen
photosynthetic	able to make food using the light from the sun
elimination	removal or destruction of something

B. Listen to the first part of a lecture. Then answer the questions. `Track 2-10`

1. What is the lecture mainly about?

_____.

2. What has happened to the coral?

_____.

3. What do you think the professor will talk about?

_____.

Now practice the questions and answers with a partner.

C. Listen and repeat. `Track 2-11`

Practice

A. Listen to the full lecture and take notes. `Track 2-12`

- Coral is _____
- Oceans _____
- Coral depends _____
- Sea temperatures _____
  _____
- This results _____
- Coral reefs _____
- Marine life _____
- It's a natural _____
- Coral can _____

B. Use your notes to complete the answers.

1. Why does the professor say that coral bleaching is occurring more often?

The professor says that coral bleaching _____
_____.

2. What reasons does the professor give for why coral reefs are so important?

The professor gives _____ as reasons
for why coral reefs are so important.

Now practice the questions and answers with a partner.

Prompt

C. Read the prompt.

> The professor discusses how coral bleaching is occurring and why coral reefs
> are important. Using points and examples from the lecture, describe the causes
> and effects of coral bleaching.

D. Listen to the sample response and complete the outline. `Track 2-13`

The lecture is about _____.

A. Coral bleaching

    1. Coral _____

    2. Temperature of _____

       • Coral bleaching _____

    3. Coral depends _____

       • Toxins _____

B. For over a hundred _____

    _____

C. Effects

    1. Fish and _____

    2. Tourism and _____

Conclusion: Coral reefs _____

    _____.

E. Now work with a partner. Take turns saying your own response using the outline from above.

Your time: _____ seconds   Your partner's time: _____ seconds

F. Fill in the blanks with the correct words.

prediction	exquisite	photosynthetic	elimination	prompts

1. Plants are the only _____ organisms to have leaves.

2. Serious progress has been made in the _____ of child labor.

3. Global warming _____ questions about pollution.

4. Weather forecasts can make an accurate _____ using radars.

5. Europe is famous for its _____ buildings.

Test

Step 1

Listen to the lecture and take notes. `Track 2-14`

- Global climate _getting warmer_
- Predicted effects _____
- Melting ice _also kill marine life_
- Animals are _getting extinct_
- Seventy frog species _extinct_
- Polar bears _+ seals n just 2 ecu_
- Recently _to have drowned_
- Rising sea levels _____
- Animals _____
- People's _homes will be destroyed_
- To reduce _change our habits_

Step 2

Read the prompt.

> The professor describes how global climate is getting warmer. Using points and examples from the lecture, describe the effects this has on the Earth.

Step 3

Create an outline for your response.

The lecture is about how global climate is getting warmer.

A. Effects
   1. Melting ice sheets _____
   2. Polar bears and seals _____
B. Rising sea levels
   1. Beaches _____
   2. Homes _____
   3. Drinking water _____
C. Melting ice and rising _____
Conclusion: A warmer climate will cause serious problems if habits are not changed.

Step 4

Write a response using your outline.

> The lecture is about _____.
> Melting ice sheets can have serious consequences. For example, _____
> _____.
> Rising sea levels mean _____
> _____.
> Melting ice sheets and rising sea levels _____
> _____.
> We must _____.

Work with a partner. Take turns saying your response. Then change partners two more times. Time yourselves!

Your time: _____ seconds   Partner one's time: _____ seconds

Your time: _____ seconds   Partner two's time: _____ seconds

Your time: _____ seconds   Partner three's time: _____ seconds

Check-up

Fill in the blanks with the correct words.

coral	errands	precious	bleaching	hassle
algae	picky	snorkel	marine	chores

1. People are _____ their teeth to make them whiter.

2. Housewives have many _____ to run before their children return home from school.

3. The WWF has created a center to promote _____ conservation.

4. _____ stones like diamonds, rubies, and emeralds are very valuable.

5. The Great Barrier Reef is famous for its beautiful _____ reefs.

6. Madonna is very _____ about the water she drinks. She only drinks one specific kind.

7. Scientists have discovered how _____ help coral cope with climate change.

8. The Gulf of Thailand is a great location to _____.

9. Children often have to do _____ such as cleaning their room, doing the dishes, and making their beds.

10. Since 2001, flying has become more of a _____ because the check-in process takes a long time.

[09] Independent

Getting Ready to Speak

A. Learn the words.

Key Vocabulary

stimulating	making a person or a part of the body more alert and aware
mundane	boring
content	satisfied; not wanting more or anything else
incredibly	beyond belief
unity	to act as one; oneness.

TOEFL® Vocabulary

challenging	difficult
ambitious	having a strong desire to have success
attain	to accomplish something
camaraderie	friendship
isolated	separated from; alone

B. Read the prompt. Then answer the questions.

Talk about your father's job.

1. What is your father's job?
My father is a _____.

2. What is the best part about your father's job?
The best part about my father's job is _____.

3. Would you be interested in a job like your father's? Why?
I would/wouldn't be interested in a job like my father's because _____
_____.

Now practice the questions and answers with a partner.

C. Listen and repeat. Track 2-15

Practice

Prompt 1

A. Read the prompt. Take turns answering the questions with a partner.

Think about a really exciting job.

1. What job do you think would be really exciting?
2. What would be the best part about the job?
3. What would be the worst part about the job?
4. Would you want this job? Why?

B. Make a list of interesting jobs with your classmates.

_____

_____

_____

_____

Prompt 2

C. Read the prompt. Then complete the answers with your own information.

Talk about values that are important to you.

What? _____ is very important to me.

Why? It is important because _____

_____.

When? A good example of this value was when _____.

How? I try to use this value by _____

_____.

Now practice your answers with a partner.

D. Make a list of values that are important in a job with a partner.

_____

_____

_____

_____

Prompt 3

E. Read the prompt. Then underline the phrases you could use in your own response.

What kind of qualities do you want in a job and why? Include specific reasons and details in your explanation.

Reasons to take a job

- earn lots of money
- place I can be ambitious
- stimulating
- good camaraderie
- being isolated
- be challenged

Sample Response and Outline

F. Listen to the sample responses and complete the outlines. Track 2-16

Sample response 1

Reason 1	Reason 2
_____	_____
_____	_____
_____	_____
_____	_____
_____	_____

Conclusion: _____
_____

Sample response 2

Reason 1	Reason 2
_____	_____
_____	_____
_____	_____
_____	_____
_____	_____

Conclusion: _____
_____

TOEFL® Vocabulary Practice

G. Fill in the blanks with the correct words.

challenging	isolated	attained	ambitious	camaraderie

1. Successful teams usually have good _____ among the players.
2. The famous author Henry David Thoreau lived _____ by himself in the woods for almost two years.
3. Younger adults who are in positions of power are usually incredibly _____.
4. Once goals are _____, new goals must be created.
5. It is very _____ to ride a unicycle.

Test

Step 1

Read the prompt.

> What kind of qualities do you want in a job and why? Include specific reasons and details in your explanation.

Step 2

Create an outline for your response.

_____

Reason 1

_____

_____

_____

_____

_____

Conclusion: _____

_____

Reason 2

_____

_____

_____

_____

_____

Step 3

Write a response using your outline from above.

I want a job that _____.

This is so important because _____

_____

_____.

It's also important because _____

_____

_____.

I must have a job that _____.

Work with a partner. Take turns saying your response. Then change partners two more times. Time yourselves!

Your time: _____ seconds   Partner one's time: _____ seconds

Your time: _____ seconds   Partner two's time: _____ seconds

Your time: _____ seconds   Partner three's time: _____ seconds

Integrated

Getting Ready to Speak

A. Learn the words.

pending	about to take place
effective	will be in operation
student loan	money borrowed for paying tuition
petition	a written request, usually made by a group and signed
awful	very bad; terrible

dean	the head of a department or school at a university
maximum	the most; highest amount/number
supplementary	extra; bonus
substantial	a lot; very big
accumulate	gain; gather; collect

B. Read the announcement. Then answer the questions.

> ### Tuition Increase
> The Dean of Students would like to announce a pending tuition increase. This is the first increase in the past five years. The maximum increase will be three percent of the current tuition. The university has recently had many new students enroll, and it needs this money to fund programs and facilities. These programs will benefit current and new students. The increase will start at the beginning of next year. Some students may need to find supplementary funds for next year. Please check at the office for your new tuition rates.

1. What will happen?
   The university will _____.

2. Why will the university do this?
   The university will increase tuition in order to_____
   _____.

3. What do you think the conversation will be about?
   I think the conversation will be about _____.

Now practice the questions and answers with a partner.

C. Listen and repeat. Track 2-17

Practice

A. Read the announcement again and underline the key information.

> ### Tuition Increase
>
> The Dean of Students would like to announce a pending tuition increase. This is the first increase in the past five years. The maximum increase will be three percent of the current tuition. The university has recently had many new students enroll, and it needs this money to fund programs and facilities. These programs will benefit current and new students. The increase will start at the beginning of next year. Some students may need to find supplementary funds for next year. Please check at the office for your new tuition rates.

Note-taking

B. Listen to the conversation and take notes. Track 2-18

Woman	Man
• Can't _____	• Thinks it's _____
• The increase seems _____	• Tuition is _____
• But it's _____	_____
• It will be _____	• Couldn't _____
_____	_____
• Already has _____	• Had to _____
_____	• Doesn't know _____
• Will take _____	_____
_____	• Will have to _____
• Will have to _____	_____
_____	• Thinks they should _____
	_____

Prompt

C. Read the prompt.

> The man expresses his opinion about the pending tuition increase. State his opinion, and explain the reasons he gives for holding that opinion.

D. Listen to the sample response and complete the outline. `Track 2-19`

The man thinks _____.

A. Tuition

　1. Is _____

B. He

　1. Couldn't _____

　2. Had _____

　3. Doesn't _____

　4. Will _____

C. He thinks the students should _____

Speaking Practice

E. Now work with a partner. Take turns saying your own response using the outline from above.

Your time: _____ seconds　　Your partner's time: _____ seconds

TOEFL® Vocabulary Practice

F. Fill in the blanks with the correct words.

maximum	dean	accumulate	substantial	supplementary

1. Most people want to _____ wealth.

2. At a university, the _____ is a very important person.

3. Most classes have a _____ number of students that can take the course.

4. Students can learn more if they have _____ study materials.

5. Usually, a promotion comes with a _____ pay increase.

Test

Step 1

> **Library Late Fine Notice**
>
> This notice is to let you know that your library books are still overdue. Please return your books as soon as possible to avoid a substantial fine. You have accumulated a fine of $25. Effective January 1ˢᵗ, the late fine maximum was increased. Your student council made this decision. The extra income will be used to pay for the new computer lab. You can pay your fine at the library information desk on the first floor. Your grade report will be withheld until payment is received.

Step 2

Listen to the conversation and take notes. `Track 2-20`

Man	Woman
• Received _____	• Thinks it seems _____ _____
• Has to _____ or _____	• Didn't know _____
	• Remembers _____ _____
• Didn't know _____ _____	• Thinks _____
• Thinks _____	• The extra money _____ _____
• Can't _____	• Strongly _____ _____
	• Thinks it's unfair _____ _____
• Thinks it's unfair _____ _____	• Can't _____ _____
• Wishes _____ _____	• Thinks _____ _____

Step 3

Read the prompt.

> The woman expresses her opinion about the change in the library's late charges. State her opinion, and explain the reasons she gives for holding that opinion.

Step 4

Create an outline for your response.

The woman is _____ .

A. The woman

    1. supported _____

    2. wants the extra _____

B. She thinks

    1. it's unfair _____

    2. students _____

Step 5

Write a response using your outline from above.

> The woman is _____ .
> She supported _____ because she wants the
> extra _____ .
> Also, she thinks it's unfair _____
> and those students _____ .

Work with a partner. Take turns saying your response. Then change partners two more times. Time yourselves!

Your time: _____ seconds   Partner one's time: _____ seconds

Your time: _____ seconds   Partner two's time: _____ seconds

Your time: _____ seconds   Partner three's time: _____ seconds

Check-up

Fill in the blanks with the correct words.

awful	effective	pending	petition	student loan
incredibly	mundane	unity	content	stimulating

1. Monkeys are _____ good at climbing trees.

2. It takes many years to pay back a _____.

3. Many people think that accountants have very _____ jobs.

4. An _____ haircut can be very embarrassing.

5. Getting a good massage can be _____ for the body and mind.

6. Policy changes are often _____ a while after they are introduced.

7. Smaller countries are often _____ with just one win in the World Cup.

8. People sign a _____ when they want an organization to change something.

9. North and South Korea should come to a peace agreement _____ negotiations.

10. The European Union is the _____ of twenty-five different European countries into one larger group.

[10] Independent

Getting Ready to Speak

A. Learn the words.

Key Vocabulary

seminar	a meeting on a specific subject
pre-made	something that is already made or prepared
assistant	a helper
lecture	to give an educational speech to someone
further	to extend

TOEFL® Vocabulary

oblige	to be required to do something
predominant	most common or main
acknowledge	to show awareness
ultimate	most important
discourse	a serious conversation

B. Read the prompt. Then answer the questions.

Talk about your perceptions of university.

1. What do you think university students are like?

   I think university students are _____.

2. How do you think professors treat university students?

   I think professors treat students _____.

3. What is the most important lesson to learn while at university?

   The most important lesson to learn at university is _____.

Now practice the questions and answers with a partner.

C. **Listen and repeat.** Track 2-21

Practice

Prompt 1

A. Read the prompt. Then take turns answering the questions with a partner.

> Talk about something that you have to do every day.

1. What do you have to do every day?
2. Why do you have to do this every day?
3. What happens to you if you don't do this every day?
4. Do you think you should have to do this every day? Why?

B. Make a list of responsibilities with your classmates.

_____

_____

_____

_____

Prompt 2

C. Read the prompt. Then complete the answers with your own information.

> Talk about something that you had to do as a child but have a choice of doing now.

What?	I had to _____.
When?	I started to be able to choose to do this when _____.
How come?	I had to do this because _____.
Why?	Now, I do/don't do this because _____
	_____.

Now practice your answers with a partner.

D. Make a list of choices that children can make with a partner.

_____

_____

_____

_____

E. Read the prompt. Then underline the phrases you could use in your own response.

> Some people think university students shouldn't have to attend every class and that attendance should be optional. What do you think? Why?

Reasons to attend or not attend classes

- waste of time
- need to read books
- end result is all that matters
- responsibility
- disrespectful
- must go to learn

Sample Response and Outline

F. Listen to the sample responses and complete the outlines. `Track 2-22`

Sample response 1

_____

Reason 1	Reason 2
_____	_____
_____	_____
_____	_____
_____	_____
_____	_____

Conclusion: _____
_____

Sample response 2

_____

Reason 1	Reason 2
_____	_____
_____	_____
_____	_____
_____	_____

Conclusion: _____
_____

TOEFL® Vocabulary Practice

G. Fill in the blanks with the correct words.

obliged	predominant	acknowledge	ultimate	discourse

1. Red is the _____ color in a sunset.
2. It is essential to have _____ on important topics so people can come to the best solution.
3. In some countries, men are _____ to join the military for a year or two.
4. For many people, being rich is their _____ goal.
5. When first entering a room, it is polite to _____ everyone.

Test

Step 1

Read the prompt.

Some people think university students shouldn't have to attend every class and that attendance should be optional. What do you think? Why?

Step 2

Create an outline for your response.

_____

Reason 1

_____

_____

_____

_____

Reason 2

_____

_____

_____

_____

Conclusion: _____

_____

Step 3

Write a response using your outline from above.

College students _____ be obliged to go to class. Going to class _____ important because _____

_____

_____.

But the predominant reason is _____

_____

_____.

Students should _____.

Extension

Work with a partner. Take turns saying your response. Then change partners two more times. Time yourselves!

Your time: _____ seconds

Your time: _____ seconds

Your time: _____ seconds

Partner one's time: _____ seconds

Partner two's time: _____ seconds

Partner three's time: _____ seconds

Integrated

Getting Ready to Speak

A. Learn the words.

Key Vocabulary

silicon	a nonmetallic element found in the Earth
microchip	a small device used to run electronics
monumental	of great importance or significance
venture capitalist	a person who invests in small companies to help them expand
explode	to blow up or to burst

TOEFL® Vocabulary

synonymous	having the same meaning
reliant	dependent
federal	pertaining to a central national government
commerce	the trade of goods and services
inhabit	to live or be found in a place

B. Read the passage. Then answer the questions.

The Birth of Silicon Valley

Silicon Valley is synonymous with computers. It is located on the southern part of the San Francisco Bay. It is also really close to Stanford University.

Silicon is an important element in making microchips. The microchip was a monumental invention that came from Silicon Valley. Modern technology is reliant upon the microchip. Because of this, hundreds of other technology firms began to form in the area. Soon Silicon Valley was making microchips, computers, and software. These companies all needed money, so venture capitalists soon came in to fund these new companies. Silicon Valley was born.

1. Which important invention came from Silicon Valley?
   The _____ was invented in Silicon Valley.
2. Why are there so many technology firms in Silicon Valley?
   There are so many technology firms because _____.
3. What do you think this lecture will be about?
   I think this lecture will be about _____.

👤👤 **Now practice the questions and answers with a partner.**

🎧 **C. Listen and repeat.** Track 2-23

Practice

A. Read the passage again and underline the key information.

The Birth of Silicon Valley

Silicon Valley is synonymous with computers. It is located on the southern part of the San Francisco Bay. It is also really close to Stanford University.

Silicon is an important element in making microchips. The microchip was a monumental invention that came from Silicon Valley. Modern technology is reliant upon the microchip. Because of this, hundreds of other technology firms began to form in the area. Soon Silicon Valley was making microchips, computers, and software. These companies all needed money, so venture capitalists soon came in to fund these new companies. Silicon Valley was born.

Note-taking

B. Listen to the lecture and take notes. Track 2-24

Location and name

- Is located _____
- Got its name from __2 places – location / what was invented here__

What was started there

- Two Stanford graduates started _____
  - Name was _____
  - Became _____
- Also worked on _____
  - Robert Noyce and Gordon Moore started _____
  - It was a _____

What else came there

- People came because _____
- Needed _____
- People became _____

Prompt

C. Read the prompt.

The professor and the passage give details about Silicon Valley. Talk about how Silicon Valley came to be synonymous with technology.

D. Listen to the sample response and complete the outline. `Track 2-25`

The lecture and the passage were about _____.

A. Name

    1. Is located on _____

    2. Got its name from _____

B. Companies

    1. Two Stanford graduates started _____

      • It became the _____

    2. Gordon Moore and Robert Noyce started _____

      • Used the _____ to start their company

      • It was a _____

C. New companies

    1. Companies soon came to Silicon Valley because _____

    2. These companies needed _____

    3. _____ gave them money

    4. People became _____

Speaking Practice

E. Now work with a partner. Take turns saying your own response using the outline from above.

Your time: _____ seconds   Your partner's time: _____ seconds

TOEFL® Vocabulary Practice

F. Fill in the blanks with the correct words.

synonymous	federal	reliant	commerce	inhabit

1. Inuit Native Americans _____ the northern parts of Canada and Alaska.

2. The business world has become _____ upon the Internet for fast communication.

3. The iPod is _____ with MP3 players.

4. The _____ government is much stronger and more powerful than city governments.

5. Even today, most _____ is done on boats and on the railroad; the same as it was done one hundred years ago.

Test

Step 1

Read the passage.

The Importance of Silicon Valley

These days, Silicon Valley is still synonymous with technology, but it has also expanded to much more than computers and microchips. These days, much of the world's electronic commerce, or e-commerce for short, is based in Silicon Valley. The world has become reliant on Silicon Valley to grow, innovate, and lead the next technology explosion. Silicon Valley has always responded well. Companies that have made monumental changes to the world all inhabit Silicon Valley. From the beginning, Silicon Valley has exploded from a computer, microchip area to one with Internet, search, venture capitalists, and high-tech science research.

Step 2

Listen to the lecture and take notes. `Track 2-26`

The second wave

- First in the second wave was _____
- It raised _____

The 1990s

- Companies such as _____
- There was a _____
- E-commerce started _____
- Ebay, Google, and Verisign allowed _____

The stock market

- American stock market became _____
- In 2000, _____
- This caused _____

Silicon Valley now

- Now it is _____
- It is growing _____

Step 3

Read the prompt.

The professor and passage talk about Silicon Valley. Explain how Silicon Valley was and will continue to be important in the future.

Step 4

Create an outline for your response.

The passage and the lecture were about _____.

A. Companies
1. Apple _____
2. Adobe, Cisco, Netscape, Yahoo _____
3. Ebay, Google, Verisign _____

_____

B. The American stock market became _____
1. Silicon Valley helped to _____
2. When Silicon Valley went down, _____
C. Now Silicon Valley _____
D. The next great wave will be in _____

Step 5

Write a response using your outline from above.

> The passage and the lecture were about _____.
> Apple _____
> _____.
> Adobe, Cisco, Netscape, and Yahoo all _____
> _____.
> Ebay, Google, and Verisign then came along and _____
> _____.
> The American stock market became _____
> _____.
> When it went down, _____.
> The next great wave in Silicon Valley will _____.

Extension

Work with a partner. Take turns saying your response. Then change partners two more times. Time yourselves!

Your time: _____ seconds   Partner one's time: _____ seconds

Your time: _____ seconds   Partner two's time: _____ seconds

Your time: _____ seconds   Partner three's time: _____ seconds

Check-up

Fill in the blanks with the correct words.

silicon	lecture	pre-made	seminars	microchip
assistant	monumental	venture capitalists	explode	further

1. Parents often _____ their children on the dangers of drugs and alcohol.

2. A _____ is inside every computer.

3. After high school, many students _____ their education by going to university.

4. _____ food that you put in the microwave is less healthy than normal food.

5. The Battle of Waterloo was a _____ victory for England because it finally defeated Napoleon and the French.

6. Companies use _____ to teach their employees new things they are trying to do.

7. It is dangerous to smoke when putting gasoline into your car because the gasoline can _____.

8. The _____ to the chef in a kitchen is called the sous-chef.

9. Small companies often go to _____ to get money to expand.

10. _____ is one of the most abundant elements in the Earth.

[11] Independent

Getting Ready to Speak

A. Learn the words.

keep in touch	to stay in contact with someone
cope	to deal with something successfully
set	a group of people or things
peer	a person who is of equal standing with another
strain	stress on the body or mind

heritage	a person's past or where they come from
solitude	the state of being alone
urban	relating to a city
resentful	a feeling of anger about something
preconceived	formed in the mind in advance

B. Read the prompt. Then answer the questions.

Talk about your hometown.

1. Do you have a lot of family and friends in your hometown?
   I have/don't have _____.
2. Do you think there are a lot of job opportunities in your hometown? Why?
   I think there _____
   because _____.
3. Do you think your town is a good place to raise a family? Why?
   I think that it _____
   because _____.

Now practice the questions and answers with a partner.

C. Listen and repeat. `Track 2-27`

Practice

A. Read the prompt. Then take turns answering the questions with a partner.

Talk about some of the people that you know in your town.

1. Who do you know that grew up in a different city than where they live now?
2. Do you think this person is happy about moving? Why?
3. Who do you know that grew up in your hometown?
4. Do you think he or she is happy for never moving? Why?

B. Make a list of reasons to move to a new city with your classmates.

_____

_____

_____

_____

Prompt 2

C. Read the prompt. Then complete the answers with your own information.

Talk about a city you visited that you really liked.

Which?   I visited _____.

When?   I visited _____ ago.

What?   The thing I liked most about this city was its _____

_____.

Why?   I would/wouldn't want to live there because _____

_____.

Now practice your answers with a partner.

D. Make a list of good things about living close to home with a partner.

_____

_____

_____

_____

E. Read the prompt. Then underline the phrases you could use in your own response.

Do you want to live near where you grew up or move away? Why? Include specific reasons and details in your explanation.

Reasons to live near where you grew up or to move away

- fresh start
- new adventures
- new peers and friends
- comfortable
- heritage is there
- miss your family

Sample Response and Outline

F. Now listen to the sample responses and complete the outlines. `Track 2-28`

Sample response 1		Sample response 2	
Reason	Examples	Reason	Examples
_____	_____	_____	_____
_____	_____	_____	_____
_____	_____	_____	_____
_____	_____	_____	_____
_____	_____	_____	_____

Conclusion: _____

Conclusion: _____

TOEFL® Vocabulary Practice

G. Fill in the blanks with the correct words.

heritage   solitude   urban   resentful   preconceived

1. Many people need to move from the countryside to more _____ areas to find good jobs.

2. It is really important to know where your family _____ comes from.

3. Siblings can sometimes be _____ of each other if they think they are being treated differently.

4. Many people need to work in _____. If there are other people around, they find it distracting.

5. You shouldn't make _____ judgements about people before you meet them.

Test

Step 1

Read the prompt.

Do you want to live near where you grew up or move away? Why? Include specific reasons and details in your explanation.

Step 2

Create an outline for your response.

_____

Reasons

_____

_____

_____

_____

Conclusion: _____

_____

Examples

_____

_____

_____

_____

Step 3

Write a response using your outline from above.

I want to live _____.

I want to do this because _____

_____

_____.

For example, _____

_____

_____.

I will follow _____.

Extension

Work with a partner. Take turns saying your response. Then change partners two more times. Time yourselves!

Your time: _____ seconds   Partner one's time: _____ seconds

Your time: _____ seconds   Partner two's time: _____ seconds

Your time: _____ seconds   Partner three's time: _____ seconds

Integrated

Getting Ready to Speak

A. Learn the words.

workload	the amount of tasks one must do
perform	to do something that has been prepared for
organizer	someone who plans and arranges an event for people
awesome	very impressive; fantastic
probable	very likely to happen

deduct	to take away a certain amount from the total
implicit	implied; unquestioning; absolute
panel	a group of people who are chosen to do something
radical	excellent or wonderful (slang)
whereby	by means of which; such that

B. Listen to the first part of a conversation. Then answer the questions. `Track 2-29`

1. What are the students discussing?

   The students are discussing _____.

2. What reasons does the student give for attending summer school?

   The student's reasons for attending summer school _____

   _____.

3. What do you think the rest of the conversation will be about?

   I think the rest of the conversation _____.

4. What do you think the student should do?

   I think the student should _____.

Now practice the questions and answers with a partner.

C. Listen and repeat. `Track 2-30`

Practice

A. Listen to the full conversation and take notes. `Track 2-31`

Man	Woman
• Can't decide _____ _____ • Will deduct _____ _____ • Spoke _____ • Summer panel _____ _____ • Can take _____ _____ • Parents _____ _____ • Feels he can _____ _____ • Still _____	• He deserves _____ • Will perform _____ _____ • Impressed _____ • Concerned _____ _____ • Says _____ _____

B. Use your notes to complete the answers.

1. What are some reasons the students discuss for attending summer school?
   The students discuss _____
   _____.

2. What reasons do the students discuss for taking a vacation?
   The students discuss _____
   _____.

Now practice the questions and answers with a partner.

C. Read the prompt.

> The students discuss attending summer school and taking a vacation. Describe the advantages of both options. Then state which option you think is best.

D. Listen to the sample response and complete the outline. `Track 2-32`

The conversation is about _____.

A. Advantages of attending summer school

    1. Will _____

    2. Graduate _____

    3. Probable _____

B. Advantages of taking vacation

    1. Studying _____

    2. Important _____

Conclusion: I think _____

            because _____.

E. Write your own conclusion using the outline from above.

Conclusion: I think _____

            because _____.

Speaking Practice

F. Now work with a partner. Take turns saying your own response using the outline from above.

Your time: _____ seconds   Your partner's time: _____ seconds

TOEFL® Vocabulary Practice

G. Fill in the blanks with the correct words.

deducts	implicit	panel	radical	whereby

1. In America, there is a law _____ all children can receive free education.
2. Risk is _____ in rock-climbing.
3. Going to the Olympics would be a _____ experience.
4. The government _____ tax from a person's salary in order to maintain the country's economy.
5. An interview _____ must ask appropriate questions to determine who will be the best candidate for a certain position.

Test

Step 1

Listen to the conversation and take notes. **Track 2-33**

Woman	Man
• Hard-earned _____ _____	• Grades _____ _____
• Grades _____ _____	• Has a radical _____
• Improve _____	• Friend _____ _____
• Earn _____ _____	• Energetic _____
• Awesome _____ _____ _____	• Great _____
	• Probable _____ _____ _____
	• Maybe _____

Step 2

Read the prompt.

> The students are discussing attending summer school or getting a job during the vacation. Describe the advantages of each option. Then state which option you would choose.

Step 3

Create an outline for your response.

The conversation is about _____.

A. Planned to

   1. Get _____

   2. Save _____

   3. Work _____

B. Probable that _____

C. Low grades

   1. Should _____

   2. Maybe _____

   3. Could make _____

Conclusion: I would prefer _____

_____.

Step 4

Write a response using your outline.

The conversation is about _____.
The student planned to _____
_____.
It's probable that _____.
His grades are low _____
_____
_____.
I would prefer to _____
_____.

Extension

Work with a partner. Take turns saying your response. Then change partners
two more times. Time yourselves!

Your time: _____ seconds   Partner one's time: _____ seconds
Your time: _____ seconds   Partner two's time: _____ seconds
Your time: _____ seconds   Partner three's time: _____ seconds

Check-up

Fill in the blanks with the correct words.

organizer	peers	perform	strain	keep in touch
workload	awesome	cope	probable	set

1. When a couple lives far away from each other, it can put a big _____ on their relationship.

2. People often find it difficult to _____ with their friends once they get older.

3. New college students often find it difficult to _____ with being away from home for the first time.

4. Students often have a massive _____ during their graduation year.

5. Group trips need a good _____ to be satisfactory.

6. Actors practice for a long time before they _____ in front of people.

7. Students often get a new _____ of friends when they go to university.

8. Scientists believe it is _____ that sea temperatures will continue to rise.

9. A sky dive is supposed to be an _____ experience.

10. Doctors often gather once a year to meet with their _____ to discuss new advances in medicine.

[12] Independent

Getting Ready to Speak

A. Learn the words.

Key Vocabulary

extensive	broad in scope; vast
marketplace	a place where things are bought or sold and ideas are exchanged
globalize	to make worldwide
employable	to have skills that make one eligible for a job
stability	the quality of not changing

TOEFL® Vocabulary

frequently	on many occasions; often
critical	extremely important
attain	to achieve something
continuity	the connection and flow within something
promotion	an advancement into a higher position, often in a job

B. Read the prompt. Then answer the questions.

Talk about your father's career.

1. How many different careers has your dad had?

   My dad has had _____ careers.

2. How many different companies has your dad worked for?

   My dad has worked for _____.

3. How long has your dad worked at his current job?

   My dad has worked at his current job for _____.

Now practice the questions and answers with a partner.

C. **Listen and repeat.** Track 2-34

Practice

Prompt 1

A. Read the prompt. Then take turns answering the questions with a partner.

> Talk about your dream job.

1. What is your dream job?
2. Do you want to work for a specific company? Why?
3. Why is this your dream job?
4. How long do you hope you will work at this job?

B. Make a list of reasons why you would change jobs with your classmates.

_____

_____

_____

_____

Prompt 2

C. Read the prompt. Then complete the answers with your own information.

> Talk about someone you know who changed jobs.

Who? _____ changed jobs.

When? He/She changed jobs _____.

How come? He/She changed jobs because _____.

Why? He/She is happy/not happy with the change because _____

_____.

Now practice your answers with a partner.

D. Make a list of good reasons to stay at a job for a long time with a partner.

_____

_____

_____

_____

E. Read the prompt. Then underline the phrases you could use in your own response.

Some people think you should change jobs often rather than staying in one job for a long time. What do you think? Why?

Reasons to stay in a job or change jobs

- get promotions
- don't have to adjust
- earn more money
- strain on family
- new challenges
- can change location

Sample Response and Outline

F. Now listen to the sample responses and complete the outlines. Track 2-35

Sample response 1

_____

Reason 1 | Reason 2
_____ | _____
_____ | _____
_____ | _____
_____ | _____
_____ | _____

Conclusion: _____
_____

Sample response 2

_____

Reason 1 | Reason 2
_____ | _____
_____ | _____
_____ | _____
_____ | _____

Conclusion: _____
_____

TOEFL® Vocabulary Practice

G. Fill in the blanks with the correct words.

| promotion | attain | frequently | continuity | critical |

1. When traveling through the desert, it is _____ to drink plenty of water.
2. Having _____ in your life allows you to establish a routine.
3. Many people will not stay at a job if there is no possibility of _____.
4. It takes many years of work and practice to _____ a black belt in Taekwondo.
5. High school students _____ send text messages to their friends.

Test

Step 1

Read the prompt.

> Some people think you should change jobs often rather than stay in one job for a long time. What do you think? Why?

Step 2

Create an outline for your response.

Reason 1

_____
_____
_____
_____

Reason 2

_____
_____
_____
_____

Conclusion: _____
_____

Step 3

Write a response using your outline from above.

I think _____.
This is so important because _____
_____
_____.
More importantly, _____
_____
_____.
It is much better to _____.

Extension

Work with a partner. Take turns saying your response. Then change partners two more times. Time yourselves!

Your time: _____ seconds   Partner one's time: _____ seconds
Your time: _____ seconds   Partner two's time: _____ seconds
Your time: _____ seconds   Partner three's time: _____ seconds

Integrated

Getting Ready to Speak

A. Learn the words.

Key Vocabulary

Broadway	a street in New York City, famous for its theaters
bear	to have as a feature or characteristic; to exhibit; to show
production	a play, movie, etc. that is produced for the public
state of affairs	the current conditions of a situation
mass media	any means of communication which can reach a large number of people

TOEFL® Vocabulary

commercial	related to business and the buying and selling of things
resemblance	being similar to something or someone
senselessness	having no good reason or purpose
prime	a period or time of peak condition
dramatically	surprisingly, quickly, or related to a drama

B. Listen to the first part of a lecture. Then answer the questions. `Track 2-36`

1. What is the lecture mainly about?

   The lecture is mainly about _____.

2. When was Broadway founded?

   Broadway was founded _____.

3. What else do you think the professor will talk about?

   I think the professor _____.

Now practice the questions and answers with a partner.

C. Listen and repeat. `Track 2-37`

Practice

Note-taking

A. Listen to the full lecture and take notes. Track 2-38

- Broadway was founded _____
- In the beginning, _____
  _____
- Audiences were _____
- World War I _____
- Broadway began _____
- Production _____
- Well known _____
- Great Depression _____
- Creative time _____
- Mass media _____
- But still _____

B. Use your notes to complete the answers.

1. How does the professor describe Broadway in the beginning?
   The professor describes Broadway as _____
   _____.

2. What events or developments does the professor discuss which brought about changes in Broadway?
   The professor discusses _____
   as events and developments which brought changes to Broadway.

Now practice the questions and answers with a partner.

Prompt

C. Read the prompt.

The professor discusses the history of Broadway. Using points and examples from the lecture, describe the major changes in Broadway.

D. Listen to the sample response and complete the outline. `Track 2-39`

The lecture is about _____.

A. Founded

    1. Shows provided _____

    2. Bore _____

      • Audiences _____

    3. Broadway supported _____

      • Theaters _____

B. After the war _____

C. 1930s

    1. Number of _____

    2. Creative and _____

Conclusion: Broadway responds to _____

_____.

E. Now work with a partner. Take turns saying your own response using the outline from above.

Your time: _____ seconds   Your partner's time: _____ seconds

F. Fill in the blanks with the correct words.

prime	dramatically	commercial	resemblance	senselessness

1. Fall is the _____ time to fish for salmon.

2. Something that sells very well is considered a _____ success.

3. Cheating on an exam is an act of _____.

4. The Chinese economy has increased _____ in the past decade.

5. Twins usually show a _____ both physically and mentally.

Test

Step 1

🎧 Listen to the lecture and take notes. **Track 2-40**

- New York is _____
- *Cats* is _____
- Composed by _____
- Performed all around _____
- Story is about _____
- *The Lion King* is _____
- It is about _____
- Musicals often use animals _____
- Theater is important _____

Step 2

Read the prompt.

> The professor describes some popular musicals on Broadway. Using points and examples from the lecture, describe how the musicals are important to people all over the world.

Step 3

Create an outline for your response.

The lecture is about popular Broadway musicals.

A. *Cats*
    1. One of longest running _____
    2. First performed in _____
B. *The Lion King*
    1. Based on _____
    2. Simba becomes _____
    3. It is about _____
C. Animals are used to _____

Conclusion: The theater is important to people, which is evident by the popularity of musicals performed all over the world.

Step 4

The lecture is about _____ .
Cats is one of the most famous musicals. It was _____
_____ .

The Lion King is also a famous musical. It is about _____
_____ .

Musicals are often written about _____ .
People all over the world _____ .

Extension

Work with a partner. Take turns saying your response. Then change partners two more times. Time yourselves!

Your time: _____ seconds   Partner one's time: _____ seconds
Your time: _____ seconds   Partner two's time: _____ seconds
Your time: _____ seconds   Partner three's time: _____ seconds

Check-up

Fill in the blanks with the correct words.

Broadway	marketplace	stability	mass media	extensive
globalized	bear	production	state of affairs	employable

1. Being able to speak a second language makes you much more _____.

2. _____ is often blamed for social problems.

3. Having a strong government may create _____ in the economy.

4. *The Phantom of the Opera* was a popular _____ musical.

5. Newspapers deal with the national and international _____ on a daily basis.

6. The Louvre Museum in Paris has an _____ collection of paintings.

7. In the _____ world, work can be done at anytime, anywhere in the world.

8. *Bee Movie* is a recent Dream Works _____.

9. Identical twins usually look almost exactly the same. However, non-identical twins may also _____ a likeness to each other.

10. Good English skills are very important to work in the international _____.

[Review 2]

Step 1

Listen to the prompt.

Everyone remembers a special time or event in their life. For some people the event is so substantial that the year it occurs is considered the best year of their life. Describe the best year of your life. State why it was so good.

Step 2

Create an outline for your response.

_____

Reason 1

_____

_____

Like to

_____

_____

Reason 2

_____

_____

Like to

_____

_____

Conclusion: _____

_____

Step 3

Write a response using your outline from above.

The best year of my life was _____.
At first, _____
_____.
_____.
I also _____
_____.
Sometimes, _____
_____.

Extension

Work with a partner. Take turns saying your response. Then change partners two more times. Time yourselves!

Your time: _____ seconds	Partner one's time: _____ seconds
Your time: _____ seconds	Partner two's time: _____ seconds
Your time: _____ seconds	Partner three's time: _____ seconds

Step 1

Read the passage.

> ### The Rise of Russian Literature
>
> Russian literature has a long and rich tradition. However, it wasn't until the nineteenth century that the works of Russian writers became known internationally. As romanticism swept through Europe, it also swept through Russia. Russian writers of this era are acknowledged for using more realistic and common themes in their stories. Many writers delved deep into the height of human suffering in Russia at that time. Russia has also produced some of the greatest novelists in world literature, and many books have been translated into several languages.

Step 2

Listen to the lecture and take notes. Track 2-41

Russian Literature
- Before the _____
- In the 1830s _____
- Resulted in _____

Dostoevsky
- *Crime and Punishment* _____
- About a poor student _____
- Uses her money _____
- She encourages _____

Themes and popularity
- Themes frequently _____
- *Crime and Punishment* _____

Step 3

Read the prompt.

> The professor talks about Russian literature since the nineteenth century. Explain the changes in Russian literature and talk about a Russian novelist.

Step 4

Create an outline for your response.

The passage and the lecture are about _____.

A. Russian literature

    1. Has a long _____

    2. Two of the _____

    3. Dealt with _____

    4. Synonymous _____

B. Dostoevsky

    1. Writer of _____

    2. About a _____

    3. She encourages _____

    4. He believes _____

Step 5

Write a response using your outline from above.

> The passage and the lecture are about _____.
>
> It has _____
>
> _____.
>
> Russia has produced _____ Tolstoy
>
> and Dostoevsky. Russian literature at that time _____
>
> _____.
>
> *Crime and Punishment* _____
>
> _____.
>
> It is about _____
>
> _____.
>
> He falls in _____
>
> _____.
>
> The young _____.

Extension

👤👤 **Work with a partner. Take turns saying your response. Then change partners two more times. Time yourselves!**

Your time: _____ seconds	Partner one's time: _____ seconds
Your time: _____ seconds	Partner two's time: _____ seconds
Your time: _____ seconds	Partner three's time: _____ seconds

Step 1

Listen to the conversation and take notes. **Track 2-42**

Female student	Male student
• Dean suggested _____	• How _____
• Will be _____	_____
• All students _____	• Study _____
• Not _____	• Need _____
• Dean said _____	• Advantages _____
_____	_____
• Think I _____	• Take _____
• Own _____	
• Good _____	
• Resolve _____	
_____	
• Good _____	
_____	

Step 2

Read the prompt.

> The students are discussing if the female student should run for student president or concentrate on her studies. Discuss the advantages and disadvantages of both options. Then state which option you would prefer.

Step 3

Create an outline for your response.

The conversation is about _____.

A. The dean has _____

B. Reasons to run for president

    1. Could cater _____

    2. Look good on _____

    3. Good _____

C. Reasons to concentrate on studies

    1. Challenging _____

    2. Own work _____

    3. Good grades _____

Conclusion: I would prefer _____.

Step 4

Write a response using your outline.

The conversation is about _____

_____.

The dean _____

_____.

She _____

_____.

However, _____

_____.

Good _____

_____.

I would prefer _____

_____.

Work with a partner. Take turns saying your response. Then change partners two more times. Time yourselves!

Your time: _____ seconds   Partner one's time: _____ seconds
Your time: _____ seconds   Partner two's time: _____ seconds
Your time: _____ seconds   Partner three's time: _____ seconds

Step 1

Read the prompt.

> Some students take time off after school and travel, and some students go straight to university. Which do you think is better? Why?

Step 2

Create an outline for your response.

_____

Reason 1
_____
_____

Reason 2
_____
_____

Better because
_____
_____

_____
_____

Conclusion: _____
_____

Step 3

Write a response using your outline.

I think students _____.
Students _____
_____.
It is important _____
_____.
I also think _____
_____.
It is more likely _____.
I would prefer _____
_____.

👤👤 **Work with a partner. Take turns saying your response. Then change partners two more times. Time yourselves!**

Your time: _____ seconds   Partner one's time: _____ seconds
Your time: _____ seconds   Partner two's time: _____ seconds
Your time: _____ seconds   Partner three's time: _____ seconds

Speaking Feedback and Evaluation Form

	The response...	0	1	2	3	4
CONTENT	addresses the question or prompt well					
	has relevant details					
	connects ideas clearly					
LANGUAGE	uses accurate grammar					
	uses appropriate vocabulary					
	has fluent speech					
	has clear pronunciation					

Total: _____ /28

Basic Skills for the
TOEFL® iBT 3

Edaan Getzel
Tanya Yaunish

Speaking

Transcript & Answer Key

Transcript

[Unit 1]

Independent

Page 7

C

W: I saw the gadget on TV. It allowed you to cut vegetables in stylish ways. The gadget didn't look useful because I never want to cut my vegetables in stylish ways.

Page 9

F

Sample response 1

M: My favorite gadget is my cell phone. It has so many handy features! It really helps me to organize my life. One of the features that are particularly useful is the daily planner. This lets me stay up-to-date with all the things that I need to do in my hectic life. My phone also helps me communicate with my friends in a variety of ways. I can text message, email, or call them. It gives me a lot of options for getting in contact with people. My cell phone is definitely my favorite gadget.

Sample response 2

W: My favorite gadget is my Tivo Box. Tivo is great because it lets me easily record a lot of things on TV. This way I never miss any of my favorite TV shows. I can do whatever I need to do and then watch them at a time that is more suitable for me. Tivo also has another feature that lets me fast forward through commercials and boring parts of a show. This way I also save time because I don't have to waste my time watching tedious commercials that usually irritate me. My Tivo Box is great.

Integrated

Page 11

C

W: The university will close the campus hospital. It is doing this in order to build a new library. I think the conversation will be about the bad results of closing the hospital.

Page 12

B

M: Did you see this notice? It was posted in the hospital.
W: No, I didn't. What does it say?
M: It says that the university wants to close the campus hospital.
W: Really? That's strange. Why?
M: They want to use the money to build a new library.
W: Well, we really do need a new library. The current library is too small, and there aren't enough facilities. It would be wonderful to have a new one.
M: Yes, but the hospital is much more important than the library. Just last week I was there because I had a high fever. The doctors there were really kind, and they helped me recover quickly.
W: You could also go to an off-campus hospital. There are some near the university.
M: This one is so convenient, though. I live in the dorms, so it's easy to go there before or after classes. Also, since I don't have a car, it would be really difficult to get to the other hospital. I don't want to ride the bus when I'm sick.
W: I guess not. I live in a house in the city, so it makes no difference to me.
M: Well, I'm absolutely furious. I am definitely going to this meeting on Friday. I want to keep the hospital open. It's really important to me and many other students. Will you come with me?
W: I would, but it doesn't really affect me . . .
M: Sure it does. If other students are sick, they can give their illnesses to you. You will be healthier if all students have easy access to a physician.
W: OK. I'll go with you.

D

W: The conversation is about closing the campus hospital so that they can use the money to build a new library. The man is very angry with the university for closing the campus hospital. He thinks the hospital is very important and convenient for students who live in the dorms. He also thinks that students will be healthier if they have access to a physician. He had to go to the hospital just last week and they helped him recover quickly. He can't go to another hospital because he doesn't have a car and he doesn't want to take the bus when he's sick. He will go to the meeting on Friday about the closing of the hospital to say what he thinks.

Page 14

Step 2

W: Hi.

M: Hi. Did you get a copy of the new medical center charges?

W: What medical center charges? The medical center is free, isn't it?

M: It isn't anymore. There have been some changes. The university didn't get enough money from the government, so they have started charging.

W: Are they charging for everything?

M: It says here you have to pay to see a doctor, and you will have to pay more for treatment and medicine.

W: That's terrible. I just went to the doctor last week because I had a high fever. I got some medicine, but I will have to buy some more because I haven't completely recovered. Now I'll have to pay more money. I can't afford that.

M: I don't think many students will be happy about this. Most students have very little money. No one is happy when the cost of the facilities go up.

W: I am sure the medical center can find the money from somewhere else. I don't think that charging the students is a good idea. I think many people will avoid going to the doctor to save money.

M: If that's true, then many people will give their illnesses to other students. I don't like that. It's not easy to do well in your classes if you are sick. It makes it hard to study.

W: Well, I'm going to go to the student union and complain. There must be something we can do about this.

M: I hope so. If lots of students are furious, maybe they will take away the charges.

W: That would be a good idea.

[Unit 2]

Independent

Page 17

C

W: I usually go to McDonald's for fast food. I eat fast food about once a week. After eating fast food, I feel full, and sometimes I even feel a little bit sick.

Page 19

F

Sample response 1

W: I don't think that fast food has a direct relationship to worsening health. I think that our lifestyle is much more important in determining our health. I think that people who eat a lot of fast food tend to have an unhealthy lifestyle. They usually don't exercise or do other things to take care of their body. However, I know some people who are very healthy and who often eat fast food. My brother is very slim but muscular. He loves eating hamburgers and French fries, but he also works out and is really healthy. Eating fast food doesn't always make your health worse.

Sample response 2

M: I think that fast food has made our health much worse. Fast food has very little nutritional value. It is loaded with salt, fat, and other preservatives that are not natural. These things make us fat and unhealthy. Fast food is dangerous for our health because it is really cheap and always available. There aren't many healthy and cheap fast food options and many people are in a hurry or cannot afford healthier food, so they are forced to eat fast food because it is cheap and convenient. This makes them much less healthy. I think fast food is the main cause of our worsening health.

Integrated

Page 21

C

M: Roman and Greek sculptures were made from bronze and marble. Sculptures were made to show the greatness of a man or an event. I think this lecture will be about how Greeks and Romans made sculptures.

Page 22

B

W: When people gather to talk about sculptures, ancient Greek and Roman sculptures often dominate the discussion. Greek and Roman sculptures are renowned throughout the world. They are some of the most intricate and elaborate works of art ever done. People travel from many places to see these beautifully preserved sculptures. The skill and attention to detail on them is amazing.

Greek and Roman sculptures are very similar. The reason for this is that the Romans copied the Greek style and skills when they made their own sculptures. The Greeks first developed the skills. Through war and trade, these skills eventually influenced the Romans. The Romans soon became skilled sculptors as well.

Sculptures were created for many reasons. Sometimes they were created to tell a story about a famous war or event. It is very hard to make a large sculpture. So they were made in different parts. The details and ornate design made them beautiful. Some of these sculptures were put on the walls of important buildings. Other sculptures were made for other reasons. Statues were displayed to honor a great man and his family. Important and powerful men had statues made of themselves. This was to show their importance and power. They were put in public places such as in parks, squares, and bathhouses.

Sculptures were made from both bronze and marble. Romans usually preferred bronze sculptures because they were much stronger, but marble statues were more easily sculpted. This made them look more realistic.

Page 23

D

M: The lecture and passage were about Ancient Greek and Roman sculptures. Ancient Greek and Roman sculptures are some of the most beautiful and intricate works of art ever made. People travel really far to see them. Greek and Roman sculptures are very similar. This is because the Romans copied the Greeks. The Greeks started it and the Romans learned it through trade and war. Sculptures were made both to tell important war stories and events as well as to honor great men. Sculptures were put on the sides of buildings, in public squares and in parks. Sculptures were also made from bronze and marble. Bronze was stronger. Marble was more easily sculpted. Marble usually looked more realistic. The Romans, though, preferred bronze statues. Greek and Roman sculptures are great.

Page 24

Step 2

M: Bronze and marble statues both have intricate and ornate details. But they are sculpted, valued, and preserved very differently.

There are not many bronze Greek and Roman statues. This is because bronze was such an important metal. Bronze is a combination of the elements tin and copper. It is light and also very strong. It allows skilled sculptors to make beautiful sculptures. Bronze was also used to make deadly weapons. Having more bronze weapons could allow one army to dominate the other. As a result, bronze sculptures were often melted down during wars. They remade the bronze into weapons. This is why there aren't as many bronze statues remaining as there once were.

Marble, though, is of no use in war. It is soft and weak. While it is bad for war, it is good for art. A thin piece of marble can break easily. The *Venus Di Milo* is perhaps the most famous example of marble breaking. She lost her beautiful arms. Many other famous marble sculptures have a missing head. The head fell because the weight of the head was too much for the neck to support. This also explains why the feet and legs of marble statues are thicker than a normal person's. This is designed this way to make sure that the legs don't break and the body doesn't fall over. Marble is taken from the ground in large blocks. A skilled sculptor then sculpts the marble into a beautiful sculpture.

[Unit 3]

Independent

Page 27

C

M: I had to decide what to eat for lunch. I wasn't happy with my decision because I didn't like the sandwich that I chose. I feel that this wasn't an important decision.

Page 29

F

Sample response 1

M: The most important decision a person makes in their life is what their major will be in college. In many countries, your course of study will often lead you to your career. This will lead to your job for the next thirty to forty years. A wrong decision might make you miserable for a very long time. It is also vital to choose a topic that you are passionate about. You must be energetic and look forward to going to work. If not, you might be gloomy and dissatisfied later on in life. Choosing a major is the most important decision you can make.

Sample response 2

W: The most important decision you can make is where you live. Each person and city is unique. It is imperative to find a city that is a close match for your personality. A city that captivates you will attract other people with similar interests. This will make it far easier to make friends. A person who likes rural areas would not be happy in New York City or Tokyo. A very cosmopolitan person would not be happy in the countryside. Choosing an ideal place to live is the most important decision a person can make.

Integrated

Page 31

B

M: Hi Lisa. You look stressed. What's the matter?
W: Yes, I am. My grandmother is ill, but I have an exam. I don't know if I should postpone the exam or take it now.
M: That's too bad. Is it serious?
W: Yes. She has a breathing disorder, and the doctor needs to operate urgently. I have been studying so hard for my exams, but now I am worried that I will be too distracted to do well.

C

W: The students are discussing if the girl should postpone her exams or not. Her Grandmother is ill and needs an operation. She has studied hard for the exam but is worried that she will be distracted and will not do well in her exam.

Page 32

A

M: Hi, Lisa. You look stressed. What's the matter?

W: Yes, I am. My grandmother is ill but I have an exam. I don't know if I should postpone the exam or take it now.

M: That's too bad. Is it serious?

W: Yes. She has a breathing disorder, and the doctor needs to operate urgently. I have been studying so hard for my exams, but now I am worried that I will be too distracted to do well.

M: Won't your grandmother be unconscious during the operation? She won't be aware of you being there or not. You are prepared for the exam now so maybe you should take it.

W: Yes, she'll be unconscious, but I have a strong bond with my grandmother. She has taken care of me since I was young. I feel that I should be there with her.

M: Then you will have to study for the exam again. You will have other exams to study for at the same time. You don't want to exert too much pressure on yourself.

W: I know, but I've studied already. I have the knowledge for this exam. It should be easy to do later without too much studying.

M: Do you know if the institute will grant or deny you a deferral?

W: They said they will grant it. I checked with student services already.

M: Well, if it's not imperative that you take it now, then maybe you could defer it. You seem too upset to do the exam, but then you can't really do anything for her anyway!

W: I know. It is so hard making a decision!

M: Well, good luck deciding, and let me know if I can do anything.

Page 33

D

W: The conversation is about whether the student should postpone her exams or not. Her grandmother is sick and needs an operation. The student is worried that she will be too distracted to do well in her exam. She also feels that she should be there with her grandmother because her grandmother took care of her when she was young. She is not sure what the best option is as she has studied hard and is prepared now. If she gets a deferral she will have to study again and may exert too much pressure on herself. I think that she should postpone her exams. She is too upset and should be with her grandmother.

Page 34

Step 1

M: Hi, how are you?

W: Hi. I'm not great to be honest. I have a sleeping disorder, and it's been really bad lately.

M: I'm so sorry to hear that. Do you think that you'll be able to take your exams next week?

W: Well, I have requested a deferral, and I'm waiting for a reply. But, I'm not certain that I should postpone the exams either.

M: How long have you been feeling so bad?

W: I often have problems sleeping. Around exam times I exert so much pressure on myself, and my condition is much worse. Last week, I collapsed in class and was unconscious for a couple of minutes.

M: It sounds like you should postpone the exams for a while. Why are you not sure that you should?

W: Well, I've always had this disorder. I have studied hard all semester and attended all my classes. If the institute grants me a deferral, I don't know if I will perform any better then either. Maybe I should take the exams and get them over with.

M: Has the doctor given you medicine? Don't you think that will help you relax and be more prepared in a few months time?

W: That's why I have requested a deferral. Hopefully, the medicine will help me relax and concentrate. Also, a break from studying might be good for me right now.

M: I guess you'll have to let the institute decide for you.

W: Yes, but I think it's imperative that I make my own decision, too. I just don't know what's best for me.

Transcript

[Unit 4]

Page 37

C

W: I have a lot of knowledge about fashion. I got this knowledge by reading fashion magazines and going shopping often. I will continue to learn about this by designing my own clothes.

Page 39

F

Sample response 1

W: I think that experience is far more important than knowledge. Any person can study and read a book. Not everyone, though, has been through the rigors of a trying event. Experience also proves that you can still succeed when things do not necessarily go as planned. Experience teaches you to avoid making the same mistake. As a student, I always preferred having teachers with experience. They always seemed to be in control. They also always knew how to teach something best. I would much rather be experienced than knowledgeable.

Sample response 2

M: I think that experience and knowledge are both important. They go hand-in-hand. An experienced person without knowledge will be unsuccessful. My grandmother is extraordinarily experienced and wise, but she cannot advise me on computer matters. Knowledge without experience can also lead to failure. Recent college graduates are bursting with knowledge, but they often find it difficult to adjust to life at work. Knowledge and experience are two different things. Creating a balance of the two will lead to success in the future. Experience and knowledge are both very important.

Integrated

Page 41

B

M: The brain is the most complex organ in the human body. It produces our every thought, action, memory, feeling, and experience. It contains more than one hundred billion nerve cells. These cells are called neurons. Our brains form a million new connections every second of our lives. The pattern and strength of the connections changes constantly and no two brains are alike. It is in these changing connections that memories are stored, habits learned, and personalities shaped.

C

M: The lecture is mainly about the brain. The brain produces our thoughts, actions, memories, feelings and experiences. I think the professor will talk about how the brain functions.

Page 42

A

M: The brain is the most complex organ in the human body. It produces our every thought, action, memory, feeling, and experience. It contains more than one hundred billion nerve cells. These cells are called neurons. Our brains form a million new connections every second of our lives. The pattern and strength of the connections changes constantly and no two brains are alike. It is in these changing connections that memories are stored, habits learned, and personalities shaped.

The human brain consists of three separate parts. The first segment is in the lower section of the brain. This is sometimes called the "brain stem." This section controls your instincts, reflexes, and basic physical functioning. When we are hungry or thirsty, the instincts in this part of the brain will let us know. This causes us to eat or drink. The second section is commonly known as the mid-brain. It lies directly above the brain stem. This part of the brain is involved in many of our feelings and emotions. It allows us to sense pain and pleasure. It also stores patterns of movement and repeated tasks. The third section takes up about eighty percent of the total brain. It is sometimes called the "neocortex" or "new brain." This part of the brain allows you to think, set goals, and solve problems. The "new brain" is still developing until about the age of twenty-one. Getting the second and third sections of the brain to work together in harmony is important for maturing into adulthood.

Page 43

D

W: The lecture is about the brain. The brain produces our every thought, action, memory, feeling and experience. The brain forms connections, which store memories and habits and shape our personalities. The pattern of connections in the brain changes constantly and no two brains are alike. The human brain has three segments. The first segment is the brain stem. It controls instincts, reflexes, basic functioning, and tells us when we are hungry or thirsty. The mid-brain allows us to sense pain and pleasure. It also stores patterns of movement and repeated tasks. The neocortex or "new brain" allows us to think, set goals, and solve problems. This part is still maturing until the age of twenty-one. The mid-brain and the "new brain" must work together to mature into adulthood. The brain is very complex and is responsible for every thought, feeling or action that we produce.

Page 44

Step 1

W: When you hear the term concussion, you think brain damage, right? Concussions are actually very common. They are also the least serious form of traumatic brain injury. The brain is made of soft tissue and is cushioned by spinal fluid. It is protected by the hard skull. When a person receives a brain injury, the brain gets tossed around. It may even bang against the skull. This can cause bruising, blood vessels to tear, and injury to the nerves.

Concussions are commonly caused through sports injuries. If you play sports such as football, boxing, and hockey, a concussion is more likely. Also, men have a higher potential for concussions than women. Some symptoms include dizziness, nausea, and loss of memory. You may even lose consciousness. In some cases, it is not always obvious.

Sometimes, players return to a game when they shouldn't. This can be serious. If the brain receives another injury, there may be long-term damage. The length of time it takes to recover from a head injury differs. It depends on how severe the injury is. Diagnosing a concussion is usually straightforward. Your doctor may ask you what seem like silly questions, such as, "What is your name?" These questions are routine. The doctor also checks your reflexes. If the injury appears to be more serious, a brain scan is often performed. This is like having your brain x-rayed. A scan is not always necessary but will quickly tell you if there is serious damage. If you play sports, don't be alarmed. Wear protective headgear and use your head!

[Unit 5]

Independent

Page 47

C

M: My hobby is playing the saxophone in a band. I spend almost thirty hours a week practicing with my band. I do my hobby in an old building near my friend's house. We can be really loud there.

Page 49

F

Sample response 1

M: I often go to the movie theater. I go there because I love watching innovative special effects. I love seeing all the incredible explosions and all the characters come to life. I love to see how the special effects have improved. I also go to the movie theater because I can hang out with lots of my classmates. We get together at the theater, talk for a while, and then go watch a movie. Afterward, we go for a coffee and criticize or compliment the movie we just saw. It's a lot of fun. I love going to the movie theater.

Sample response 2

W: I often go to my grandma's nursing home. My grandma is very old, and it is hard for her to leave the nursing home, so I try to go there and visit with her as often as I can. My grandma and I have a lot in common. We always discuss politics and the articles in that day's newspaper. I also go there to volunteer on the weekends. Some of the people have family who live far away. They are lonely and want to talk to other people. I enjoy it, and I think it makes them feel better, too.

Integrated

Page 51

C

M: The announcement says that the dorm is changing its "quiet hours" because many residents are unhappy with the current "quiet hours." I think the conversation will be about how the students feel about the new hours.

Page 52

B

M: Hi. Do you want to come to my party on Thursday night? It's going to be a lot of fun.

W: I have a test on Friday, so I can't. Maybe I'll come next time. Just make sure your party ends early enough.

M: Early enough for what?

W: This building's "quiet hours" have changed. Now, we all have to reduce noise starting at 10:00 p.m. instead of 11:00 p.m. Also, the "quiet hours" end at 6:00 a.m. and not 5:00 a.m.

M: Really? I wonder why they changed. I guess a lot of social events will be victim to these new hours. It's going to be difficult to be quiet so early.

W: There are definitely pros and cons to the new system, but I'm optimistic about it. I think that these changes will create a more stable environment for studying. I have a lot of trouble studying when other people are making a lot of noise.

M: Don't you think there should be some flexibility, though. 10:00 p.m. seems really rigid. They should have different hours on weekends.

W: I don't think so. I think there are a lot of people who have part-time jobs, sports, and other things early on the weekend. Some students even have classes. I know that I like to get a good-night's sleep before I go to work on Saturday. I'm sure others feel this way, too. People can still have parties and socialize. They just need to be aware of the other residents and respect their rights.

Page 53

D

W: The woman is optimistic about the new "quiet hours." She thinks there are pros and cons to the new policy, but she is mainly optimistic as she believes it will enable a better environment for studying. At the moment, she has trouble studying when it's noisy. She also likes to sleep well before she goes to work on Saturdays and knows that other students have jobs and do sports on the weekend. So she also likes that the quiet hours happen on the weekends, too. She thinks the other students can still have fun they just need to be aware of others and be respectful to those who need the quiet time to study or sleep.

Page 54

M: Did you just post this notice on the door?

W: Yes, I did. It's about the dorm guest policy. There have been a lot of complaints, so the "guest hours" are changing.

M: Are they becoming longer or shorter?

W: Guests will be allowed in the dorm for a shorter time. They will have to leave earlier in the evening in order to allow students to have peace and quiet.

M: That's a great idea. I know that sometimes it can get really noisy around here. I have had many assignments fall victim to noise in the halls. It makes it really hard to concentrate when there are so many people around.

W: Well, some students will probably complain about the new policy. They feel that there should be more flexibility in our policy. However, I'm optimistic that the overall response to the new policy will be good.

M: There are definitely pros and cons to a policy like this, but I'm really happy about this. I think that it is going to make people more aware and more respectful of their neighbors.

W: Yes, and it will reduce the number of arguments among the residents. The rules are very strict, and there will be no exceptions. This means that everyone has to follow the same rules, and everyone will be treated equally.

M: That's great. It will bring a lot of peace to our living environment, and I think the majority of the students will be happier.

[Unit 6]

Independent

Page 57

C

W: I go shopping at Target most often. I go shopping there because it is cheap, and they have both clothes and food. I prefer shopping at big stores because they have a lot of things for me to look at and buy.

Page 59

F

Sample response 1

W: I think that it is better to shop at an independent store. This type of store is owned and operated by locals. You are supporting your own community by buying there. This makes sure that the money stays in your community. You are also helping the people who work at the store. This is done by helping to pay their salary and increasing their standard of living. A big chain store will often pay its employees a much lower salary. Shopping at the independent stores helps to make your community stronger. This is because you are directly helping people in your community more.

Sample response 2

M: I don't think that it matters where you choose to shop. The most important thing is to choose the place that gives you the best bargains. Everyone works hard for his or her money. They should spend their hard-earned money wisely. If an independent store gives the best deal, then you should shop there. Every store is competing for your business. So it is very important that they do everything that they can to give you the best deals. In the end, the more money you have in your pocket, the happier you are going to be.

Integrated

Page 61

C

M: Refugees have to flee because there is often fighting in their homeland, and they must leave, or they might be killed. They face many problems in the new countries like learning new languages, currencies, customs, and adjusting to a new way of life. I think this lecture will be about how refugees adapt to their new homeland.

Page 62

B

W: African refugees have become more common in western countries. Some parts of Africa had corrupt regimes that were at war. There also wasn't enough food. This caused people to flee their homeland. They are often minorities. They feel they must leave or be killed so they become refugees. They hope to start a new life in a new land.

Many refugees end up in Europe and America. Living in these places are very different from living in Africa. They face many problems that are inherent in a new country. The first and biggest problem for them is often communication. Many cannot speak the local language. They overcome this by taking intensive classes. They study hard because they must.

They also find a big change in weather. These countries are much colder than Africa. Some places get a lot of snow in the winter. Many of the refugees have never seen snow. They go and buy jackets and warm blankets. Often they adjust well to the new weather.

Organizations also help refugees. They help them to find jobs. There are also other African refugees in their city. They help each other adjust to the many cultural variables of life in a new land. They may learn to drive or to shop at the supermarket. They even start to root for the local sports team. Eventually, they feel as comfortable in their new home as they did in their old one, but they always remember their homeland.

Page 63

D

M: The lecture and the passage were about how refugees adjust to life in a new homeland. They have to leave because their governments are corrupt and at war. Their homelands don't have enough food, or they are worried that they will be killed. They face many problems in their new homes. They often cannot communicate. The weather also is a big change for them, but they adjust. There are other refugees and organizations that help them to adjust. They help them to find jobs and other useful things. They help to teach them important skills like driving and shopping at the store. In the end, they learn to drive and shop at the supermarket just like anyone else.

Page 64

Step 2

W: In 2003, war started in Iraq. There was a regime in power that many felt was corrupt and evil. This regime was defeated, but intensive fighting continued after the regime was defeated. This fighting made Iraqis flee their homes. Millions of people left.

Fortunately, the neighboring countries allowed Iraqis in. The Iraqi minority in all these countries is huge. They come to their new cities with their own culture. Iraqis speak a slightly different form of Arabic than their neighbors. Many Iraqis also have a different religion. They also have their own food. They bring these things into their new country.

They do things that make their new home feel more comfortable. Parts of Damascus are now called "Little Baghdad." This area feels like Iraq.

Iraqis do their best to adjust to their new homes. They start Iraqi restaurants. They start their own Mosques so they can pray. They live in groups. This lets them communicate easily.

Iraqis remember their homeland best through the theater. The Iraqis have a long history in the theater. Iraqi actors and actresses perform plays. They show the problems inherent in their new lives. The plays are often funny. The end of the play usually has a surprise. They often end sadly. They enjoy these plays. This is because they share many of the same feelings.

[Review 1]

Integrated 1

Page 68

Step 2

M: Did you hear that they lowered the grade requirements for studying abroad?

W: Yeah, I did. You seem excited.

M: Well, I am. This means that I can go study next summer in Austria. I can finally go and study music in Vienna. I've been working so hard to try to get my grades high enough. Sadly, I haven't been able to do it. I was starting to worry that I would never get the opportunity to go.

W: Well, I am really happy for you. There are pros and cons of doing this, though.

M: Not necessarily. Doing this will give opportunities for a lot more students to go abroad and experience different cultures. They will gain knowledge, become more cosmopolitan, or maybe even find something they want to study further.

W: You're right, but I think an opportunity like this should be a reward for years of hard work. It shouldn't be something that anyone can do. It is imperative for the school to grant great opportunities like studying abroad to people who really work hard for this.

M: I see your point, but it is such a great opportunity that the school shouldn't deny any student that wants to do it.

W: Maybe I'm in the minority on this, but I think the levels were good as they were. But don't get me wrong, I'm really happy for you.

M: Thanks. Let's go to the office and get some information on Austria.

W: Sounds good.

Integrated 2

Page 70

W: Many people think the mouth is only for eating, but there are many parts to the mouth. The tongue and teeth are important for communication. It is important to take good care of your mouth. Proper treatment and care will ensure you have a healthy mouth.

The first thing most people do when they meet someone new is give a warm smile. A nice smile can captivate someone. Most people's reflexes will have them smile back. A warm smile lets people relax. It can enable the start of a good relationship. A smile uses every part of the mouth.

The tongue is extraordinarily important for communication. The tongue is very muscular. It is one of the strongest muscles in the body. It can move in many different directions. These intricate movements help to make speech possible. The tongue also helps to control the air.

The teeth are also imperative to communication. The teeth are important in determining how much air passes through the mouth. They also enable us to make sounds like "th." These sounds are really important in English.

Communication is so important to how we live. Therefore, physicians always tell us to take care of our mouths. If we fail to preserve our teeth, we can lose them. This makes communication very difficult. It also makes it harder to give a beautiful smile. Even though it is sometimes tedious, it is imperative to brush and floss our teeth every day.

Transcript

[Unit 7]

Page 73

C

W: I live in Denver, Colorado. My city is located in the middle of America. It is very close to the Rocky Mountains. My city is famous for its beautiful mountains and incredible skiing.

Page 75

F

Sample response 1

M: I love almost everything about my hometown, but I hate the weather there. The weather always limits me in what I can do. I like to go outside and be active. The problem is that it always seems to be raining, or it is windy or too cold. The weather often messes up my weekend plans. Last weekend, I was planning to go canoeing with some friends, but there was a huge storm, and I had to stay inside all weekend. You can change or avoid many things in a city, but you can't modify the weather! The weather in my city often ruins my plans.

Sample response 2

W: The thing I dislike the most about my city are the terrible traffic jams. During rush hour, my commute home from work can take over an hour. Without traffic, it only takes twenty minutes to get to work. Sitting in traffic is really dull. I could leave earlier in the morning, but that would force me to get up too early. I really wish that the city officials would make resolving this problem a priority. Perhaps they could construct new roads so that the traffic could flow much smoother. It looks like I am going to be sitting in traffic everyday for a while.

Integrated

Page 77

B

W: So, do you think you will live on campus next year?
M: I'm not sure. I was thinking of buying a car, and then I could continue to live on my parents' estate.
W: Why would you want to do that? You would have much more freedom living on campus.
M: That's true, but my parents are pretty good. I could still have fun and have my own car.

C

M: The students are discussing if he should buy a car to get to university or stay on campus. The student says that his parents are good and that if he lives at home, he can still have fun and also buy a car. I think the rest of the conversation will be about why he should live on campus. I think he should stay on campus.

Page 78

A

W: So, do you think you will live on campus next year?
M: I'm not sure. I was thinking of buying a car so I could continue to live on my parents' estate.
W: Why? You would have more freedom living on campus.
M: That's true, but my parents are pretty good. Plus my older brother lives at home, and they like that. I think they would be upset if I deviated from what they think is normal. But there are other things.
W: Like what?
M: I want to enjoy university life, but it's intrinsic that I study hard. If I live on campus, there may be too many distractions. I also like the idea of having my own car.
W: Well, you seem certain that staying at home and buying a car is the best option.

M: Absolutely not. Living on campus sounds good too! If I live on campus, I will be closer to the university. I won't need to consider travel time. And I would be able to select my own room. At the moment, I have the smallest room.

W: Plus it will give you a different scope on being a student.

M: What do you mean?

W: You will have to be more independent. Your parents won't have breakfast waiting for you every morning.

M: Yes, that's true. My parents couldn't tell me what to do. Also, my brother sometimes treats me like his subordinate and that causes a lot of tension!

W: What are the living standards on campus?

M: They're tremendous! There is Internet access in each room. There is also a gym, a new library, and the food is delicious.

W: Well, what are you going to do?

M: Both choices are great, but I don't know which I want more.

Page 79

D

M: The conversation is about buying a car to get to university or staying on campus. The advantages of buying a car are that the student can continue to live on his parents' estate. His parents are good so he can have fun and still have a car. He also likes the idea of having his own car to drive to wherever he wants to go. The students also discuss the advantages of living on campus. There will be no travel time living on campus. The student also thinks that the facilities on campus are tremendous. For example, there is Internet access in all rooms, a gym and a library. I think he should live on campus. He will have more time to study and great facilities.

Page 80

Step 1

M: So are you looking forward to university life?

W: Absolutely, except that I can't decide if I should live with my parents or on campus?

M: What do your parents want you to do?

W: My mom's very easy going. She thinks that I should live on campus, but my dad would prefer that I live with them on the estate.

M: I think that living on campus is an intrinsic part of student life. It's the ideal situation by far.

W: I'm sure it's a great experience, but I don't know if it's that ideal. Living at home will be much cheaper, and the living standards are superior to campus accommodation.

M: I'm afraid I'll have to disagree with that. Campus accommodation has improved greatly. All rooms on campus now have wireless Internet access. There is a laundry service, and you will have so much freedom. Plus, you don't have a car, and if you live at home, you will need to ride a bus to class.

W: Yes, I know it will take up a tremendous amount of time traveling from home each day.

M: Well, if you live on campus, you could use that extra time to get a part-time job.

W: I don't really plan to get a part-time job. That's just a distraction. If I want to succeed, I will need to use all my free time to study.

M: Don't forget to make time for fun too.

W: I won't. Thanks for your advice. It's good to get someone else's scope on things. Now I just need to select what will be the best for me.

M: No problem. I'm sure you'll make the right decision.

Transcript

[Unit 8]

Page 83

C

W: My favorite food is lasagna. My mom makes this food best. My mom's lasagna is the best because she knows exactly all the things that I like in it.

Page 85

F

Sample response 1

W: I think that it is much better to eat at home than it is to eat at restaurants. Eating at home makes all the family come together to have dinner. This can be used to spend precious time together as a family. Thereby, ensuring that everyone is intimately involved in each other's life. Eating out can also take a long time. Going to the restaurant, ordering, eating, and then coming home can take longer than expected. Children are busy with homework and other pursuits. Parents also have important errands and other chores to do at night. So, I think eating at home is better.

Sample response 2

M: I think it is better to eat dinner at restaurants. Eating at restaurants is much easier. There is no preparation both before and after the meal. A family just has to go and eat. The restaurant takes care of everything else. Restaurants can also cater to each member's specific tastes. Even a family member who is a very picky eater can usually find something on the menu that he or she likes. Going to restaurants allows everyone to eat exactly what they want. Because it is much less of a hassle, I think it is better to go to restaurants for dinner.

Integrated

Page 87

B

M: OK class, imagine you are on an exquisite tropical island. You've packed your fins, mask, and snorkel. You go to explore the beautiful coral beneath the ocean, but instead, you find that the coral is dead. This is occurring more and more often. It is because the Earth's oceans are becoming warmer. So coral bleaching is becoming more widespread. This prompts the question: Can coral survive the bleaching?

C

M: The lecture is mainly about coral. The coral is dying. I think the professor will talk about what is causing the coral to die.

Page 88

A

M: OK class, imagine you are on an exquisite tropical island. You've packed your fins, mask, and snorkel. You go to explore the beautiful coral beneath the ocean, but instead, you find that the coral is dead. This is occurring more and more often. It is because the Earth's oceans are becoming warmer. So coral bleaching is becoming more widespread. This prompts the question: Can coral survive the bleaching?

Coral is in fact animals. They depend on algae for food. The algae live within the coral. They give the coral its bright, beautiful colors. Over the past one hundred years, sea temperatures have been rising. And there are predictions that the temperatures will continue to rise.

Rising water temperatures block the photosynthetic reaction that converts carbon dioxide into sugar. This results in a buildup of toxins. The toxins poison the algae and force the coral to reject it. As a result, the coral has no color. It is bleached white.

Coral reefs are important to snorkelers and divers. They are also important for many other reasons. They are home to hundreds of thousands of marine life and fish. If the coral continues to die, some of the marine life may become extinct. The elimination of coral reefs would also result in other great losses. The income from tourism and fishing would go down. It may also hinder the discovery of new medicines.

Coral bleaching is a natural process. However, it has been shown that stress caused by pollution and solar radiation can also result in coral bleaching. The coral can recover but only if sea temperatures become cooler.

Page 89

D

W: Coral reefs are dying more and more often. Sea temperatures are becoming warmer. Coral bleaching is more widespread. Coral depends on algae for food. The algae gives it its color. For over one hundred years, sea temperatures have been rising. This causes a buildup of toxins and poisons the algae. Fish and marine life depend on the coral. They may become extinct. Coral is important to snorkelers. Tourism and fishing will be affected by coral bleaching. They will experience a loss of income. It may also hinder the discovery of new medicines. Pollution and solar radiation are dangerous to coral. Coral reefs are very important. It is important to save them. They can be recovered if sea temperatures become cooler.

Page 90

Step 1

W: For several years, there has been growing evidence that the global climate is steadily getting warmer. Some of the predicted effects are rising sea levels and melting of glaciers. This can have serious consequences. Warmer seas kill coral. Melting ice sheets also kills marine life in colder regions. Extinction of some animals is happening quicker than predicted. At least seventy species of frogs have become extinct. Other animals that depend on the cold may be eliminated too. Polar bears and seals are just two examples.

They depend on sea ice for food and giving birth. Recently polar bears have drowned. Polar bears can swim long distances. When they need to rest, they usually do so on sea ice. There was no sea ice so the polar bear drowned as it was too tired to swim farther.

As the ice sheets melt, sea levels rise. This means that many beaches will be lost. Animals and birds living in the beach areas will also be in danger. People's homes will be destroyed. They will have to move and it will be very expensive. People living on islands will have less drinking water because of the sea salt. Millions of people will be affected.

Rising sea levels and melting ice are natural. To reduce the impacts of climate change, we need to change our habits. We need to do this as soon as possible. The longer we wait the less effective change will be.

[Unit 9]

Independent

Page 93

C

M: My father is a TV broadcaster for sports games. The best part about my father's job is the free tickets to all the big games. I wouldn't be interested in a job like my father's because he has to travel a lot and doesn't get to spend a lot of time at home.

Page 95

F

Sample response 1

M: I want a job that is challenging and stimulating. Jobs that are too easy and too routine become very mundane. A job is something that you need to do everyday for a very long time. A boring job will lead to a boring life. People who really enjoy their jobs, though, don't view their job as work. They view their jobs as recreation. Jobs that are challenging let you feel as if you have accomplished something everyday. They let you go home feeling proud and content with your day's work. A challenging and stimulating job is what I want to have.

Sample response 2

W: I want a job where I have great colleagues. We all spend so much time at work. Because of this, it is very important to get along well with your colleagues. Good colleagues can make the time pass quickly because you are enjoying yourself at work. They are also incredibly dependable. This makes people work harder and achieve even more ambitious goals. When these goals are attained, there is a great sense of camaraderie and unity. This is shared by everyone who worked together on the project. People without good colleagues often feel isolated. Great colleagues can make a job great.

Integrated

Page 97

C

W: The university will increase tuition at the beginning of next year in order to pay for programs and facilities for new students. I think the conversation will be about the possible new programs and facilities.

Page 98

B

W: I can't believe this.

M: What is it?

W: There's an announcement in the student newspaper. It's from the Dean of Students. The university has decided to increase tuition, and the increase is effective next year.

M: Really? How much will the increase be?

W: It says the maximum will be three percent. It seems small, but that's a substantial increase.

M: That's terrible. Tuition is already too high for most students to afford. Why are they increasing it?

W: Apparently, there hasn't been an increase in a really long time. With all the new students over the past few years, the university needs to update its facilities and programs. The article says that it will be good for all the students who study here.

M: I think this is terrible. I almost couldn't pay my tuition this year. I had to get a job. I don't know how I'll pay more next year. I guess I'll have to work more hours at my part-time job.

W: Yeah. I've already accumulated a lot of debt in university. Next year, my student loan will be even bigger. It will take me years to pay it back.

M: I wonder if we can stop the increase? Maybe we should start a petition or something.

W: I don't think that would work. It sounds like it's already been decided. I guess we'll have to figure something out.

M: I might have to call my parents and ask for money. I really don't want to do that.

W: This is awful.

Page 99

D

M: The man thinks tuition is already too high. He couldn't afford to pay it this year, so he had to get a job. He doesn't know how he'll pay for the tuition increase. He will have to work more hours. As a result, he thinks the students should start a petition to stop the increase.

Step 2

W: Hi. What's that you're reading? You don't look very happy about it.

M: It's a letter I received from the library about my overdue books. It says that I have to pay twenty-five dollars, or they won't give me my grade report.

W: Really? That seems like a lot of money. I didn't know that the library's late fees were so expensive.

M: Well, it says here that the fines were increased this year. I didn't even know they were thinking about raising the fines.

W: Oh, I remember now. Last fall there was a petition among the students about the library late fees. The increase in late fees was supposed to supply supplementary income for the new computers.

M: Yes, that's it exactly. I think this is awful. It's so much money. I can't afford to pay all these fees.

W: I think it's great. The extra money will really help make the new computer lab a good place to work. I strongly supported the petition because I want the new facilities to be up-to-date.

M: But what about the students who have to pay the late fees? It's unfair to expect us to pay for the new computers.

W: No, it isn't. I think it's unfair when students don't return library materials on time. If you have a book that I need and you return it late, I can't get my research done. As a result, my grades might be lower. You should be punished for disrespecting the other students.

M: Well, I wish I had returned my books on time.

[Unit 10]

Independent

Page 103

C

W: I think university students are very independent and hard working. I think professors treat students like adults with a greater sense of camaraderie. The most important lesson to learn at university is how to take care of yourself.

Page 105

F

Sample response 1

W: I think that university students should not be obliged to go to class. The predominant purpose of college is to prepare students to be adults. Students need to be allowed to make decisions for themselves. Choosing to go to class is an important choice that students need to be given. In addition, many college classes are seminar classes. These have pre-made notes and large class sizes. They also have a teacher assistant lecturing. Students can get the notes from friends and the teacher won't even notice. This is a waste of time. College students should not be obliged to go to class.

Sample response 2

M: I think that college students should be obliged to go to class. I acknowledge that they are adults and can make their own decisions, but after university, they get jobs. Everyone is obliged to go to work everyday. This is a good way to practice for the real world. More importantly, the ultimate goal of college is to get more knowledge. You learn by going to class. It also allows you to be a part of discourse with classmates. This can help to further your knowledge. College students should be obliged to go to class.

Integrated

Page 107

C

M: The microchip was invented in Silicon Valley. There are so many technology firms in Silicon Valley because modern technology is reliant upon the microchip. I think this lecture will be about how Silicon Valley started and what it is.

Page 108

B

W: Today when people hear the term Silicon Valley they think of technology. Silicon Valley is not the name of an actual valley. It is a term used to define a region of Northern California. Silicon Valley sits on the southern part of San Francisco Bay. It is near the city of San Jose.

Silicon Valley got its name from two places. One is from its location. The other is from what was invented there. The federal government used this area to test important technology after World War II. Stanford University also needed more space. It had too many students. They put them in the area.

Two Stanford graduates named William Hewlett and David Packard then started a computer company there. This company became Hewlett-Packard. It soon became the biggest computer company in the world.

People also began working on the microchip at this time. They learned that microchips work best with silicon. Robert Noyce and Gordon Moore later started the company Intel.

The microchip was a monumental invention. All technology now uses the microchip. The microchip attracted lots of smart people to the area. The area soon exploded with technology and commerce. Hundreds of new companies started to inhabit Silicon Valley.

These companies needed money. Venture capitalist firms began to set up in Silicon Valley. They put money into these companies. Many companies grew and grew. Lots of people got really rich.

Page 109

D

M: The lecture and the passage were about Silicon Valley. Silicon Valley is located on the southern part of the San Francisco Bay. It got its name from two things. One was from its location, the other from what was invented there. Many Stanford graduates started businesses in this area. Two of them started a company called Hewlett-Packard. It soon became the biggest computer company in the world. People were also working on the silicon microchip. This was a monumental invention. Robert Noyce and Gordon Moore used this invention to start the company Intel. Soon companies quickly came because modern technology is reliant upon the microchip. Other companies set up. These companies needed money to grow. They got money from venture capitalists. People became really rich.

Page 110

Step 2

M: Silicon Valley is still synonymous with the microchip. However, Silicon Valley is now also synonymous with other kinds of technology. Intel and Hewlett-Packard were the original big technology firms, although later other huge technology firms began to inhabit Silicon Valley as well.

The first in the second wave of technology was Apple. Apple was able to raise over one billion dollars from investors. This caused the venture capitalists to start their own investment companies.

The 1990s saw the Internet explode. Companies such as Netscape, Yahoo, Adobe, Cisco, and Oracle all led to a long period of growth. It was one of the greatest economic growth periods in history. E-commerce also started to grow. Companies like E-bay, Google, and Verisign all started there. They allowed people to search for an item, buy that item, and pay for the item all on the Internet.

The success of these companies led to the American stock market becoming reliant upon Silicon Valley. Silicon Valley went through a difficult time in 2000. There were too many companies. This caused a huge decrease in their values. This caused a big decrease in the American stock market.

Now, Silicon Valley is doing well again. It continues to innovate and conduct commerce. It continues to be involved in technology. But it is also growing into medicine. Technology and medicine have combined. This will create the next great wave in Silicon Valley. No one knows which company will explode next.

[Unit 11]

Page 113

C

W: I have a lot of family and friends in my hometown. I think there aren't a lot of job opportunities because people always have to move to find a job. I think that my hometown is a great place to raise a family because it is very safe.

Page 115

F

Sample response 1

M: I want to live close to where I grew up. If I move far away, it will be very hard to keep in touch with all my relatives. I couldn't cope with that. I would have to find a whole new set of peers in both my personal and professional life. My hometown is where my family heritage comes from. I'd be in solitude in a far away city. My cousin moved to Europe. He lived there for five years, but moved back home. He said he missed his family and friends. The same thing would happen to me, so I'll live close to home.

Sample response 2

W: I want to live far away from home. There are so many new challenges for me in a more urban city. I am very resentful of people from my hometown still treating me like I am still a child. I want to live where there are no preconceived ideas of who or what I am. Plus, with technology, it doesn't put a strain on my relationships with my friends and family. I can call them often. Two years ago, I moved to a new continent. I love it here and don't know when I will go back home. I like being far away from home.

Integrated

Page 117

B

M: I can't decide if I should go to summer school or take my vacation time.
W: Why would you go to summer school? You've worked hard all year and deserve the break.
M: I know I do, but if I attend summer school, it will deduct a huge amount from my workload next year. Then, hopefully, I can graduate early.
W: Don't you think that it's implicit that you have a break from studying? You will perform much better in the final exams if you take a vacation.

C

W: The students are discussing if the man should go to summer school or take a vacation. The man says that summer school will decrease his workload next year and then he can graduate early. I think the rest of the conversation will be about why he should take a vacation.

Page 118

A

M: I can't decide if I should go to summer school or take my vacation time.
W: Why would you go to summer school? You've worked hard all year and deserve the break.
M: I know I do, but if I attend summer school, it will deduct a huge amount from my workload next year. Then, hopefully, I can graduate early.
W: Don't you think that it's implicit that you have a break from studying? You will perform much better in the final exams if you take a vacation.
M: Maybe. I've spoken with the organizer of the summer school, and she told me that this year's panel of teachers are very energetic. I think they will make summer school enjoyable.
W: More enjoyable than a vacation?

M: Maybe not, but if I graduate from school early, then I can take a long vacation before I start university.

W: That would be awesome. Would you take a trip?

M: Well, my parents have a radical trip planned to Europe for next year. They've promised that I can go too if I graduate early.

W: Wow! That will be a hard-earned vacation. Don't you want to spend more time with your friends before we all go away to university?

M: Sure I do. It's probable that I can graduate early enough, whereby I can go to Europe and still spend time with my friends.

W: Do you think it's possible that you can do it all? You're putting yourself under a lot of pressure.

M: I sure hope so. I still have to decide what I will do.

Page 119

D

M: The conversation is about whether the student should attend summer school or take a vacation. The student says that attending summer school will deduct from his workload next year. He may also be able to graduate early. If he graduates early, his parents have promised to take him on a radical trip to Europe. He thinks it's probable that he can graduate early, go to Europe, and still spend time with friends. However, there are advantages to taking a vacation. If you have been studying hard all year, it is implicit to take a break from studying in order to perform better in exams. It is also important to spend time with friends before school finishes and everyone goes away to university. I think he should take the vacation time and spend as much time with friends as possible.

Page 120

Step 1

W: So, what did your parents want to talk to you about last night?

M: They wanted to talk about my grades. My average is low, and they think it's implicit that I attend summer school during the vacation.

W: But, didn't you plan on getting a job?

M: Yes, that's what I have been planning. I have a radical job lined up, working on a fruit farm. One of my friends is a great organizer. He has planned a road trip at the end of the summer, and I was going to save money to go with him.

W: That would be a hard-earned road trip. Do you know how difficult working on a farm is?

M: I'm an energetic person. It would be great working outdoors in the summer—beautiful blue skies, fresh air, and sunshine.

W: You're right about that, but if your grades are low, maybe you should listen to your parents and go to summer school. It will really improve your chance of getting into a good university.

M: I could really do with some extra studying. It's probable that I won't get any university offers with my current grades.

W: And you'll probably earn very little working on a fruit farm. I hear that they deduct money if you eat too much fruit.

M: Oh, maybe I wouldn't save very much money.

W: I have an awesome idea. Maybe you could make a deal with your parents whereby you go to summer school, and they pay for your road trip.

M: That would be great, but I'm not sure that they'll go for it.

[Unit 12]

Independent

Page 123

C

W: My dad has had three different careers and has worked for about five or six different companies. He has worked at his current job for over eight years.

Page 124

F

Sample response 1

W: I think people should try to change jobs frequently. The world is rapidly changing. Technology changes everyday. Thus, it is critical that people have an extensive range of skills and experiences, so they are better able to adapt to the changing marketplace. The best way to attain these skills is through work. Working a wide range of jobs will help employees get the skills and experience that are needed in a globalized marketplace. Frequently, changing jobs helps people to be more employable later on in life.

Sample response 2

M: It is better to stay at the same job for a long time. Staying at the same place allows you to have continuity and stability in your life. Other people might depend on your income. Having a good stable job will ensure that you and your family won't feel a lot of stress. In addition, it allows you better chances for promotion. This will allow you to work at the same place, but it gets you a better job with more responsibility and more money. Staying at the same job for a long time is what I want to do.

Integrated

Page 127

B

M: Broadway is located in central Manhattan in the US. It was founded in the early 1900s. Since then it has been the heart of commercial culture. In the beginning, the shows were funny. They provided light entertainment to people. They bore no resemblance to daily life. They attracted audiences interested in music, excitement, and romance. The audience often became involved in the shows. The orchestra had even been known to play to them after the shows.

C

M: The lecture is mainly about the shows on Broadway. Broadway was founded in the early 1900s. I think the professor will talk about how Broadway has changed.

Page 128

A

M: Broadway is located in central Manhattan in the US. It was founded in the early 1900s. Since then it has been the heart of commercial culture. In the beginning, the shows were funny. They provided light entertainment to people. They bore no resemblance to daily life. They attracted audiences interested in music, excitement, and romance. The audience often became involved in the shows. The orchestra had even been known to play to them after the shows.

When World War I began, Broadway gave support to the soldiers. Theaters were built and were used to raise money for the war. After the war, Broadway changed. It began to deal more with social and political issues. Some shows highlighted the senselessness of war. During this time, Broadway reached its prime. The number of productions grew dramatically. It also became well known for its bright lights and crowds. A French novelist remarked, "In Forty-Second Street, it is a glowing summer afternoon all night."

The Great Depression hit the US in the 1930s. Broadway, of course, took a fall, too. The number of productions dropped. Many actors were put out of work. However, this seems to have been a creative time for writers. Interesting plays were written about the American state of affairs.

Broadway has always responded to national crises and changes in society. Even though it could not compete with mass media, Broadway has always supported new ideas and continues to be an important aspect of American culture.

Page 129

D

W: Broadway was founded in the 1900s in Manhattan. In the beginning, shows provided light entertainment. The shows bore no resemblance to real life. Audiences enjoyed music, entertainment, and romance. They often became involved in the shows. The orchestra sometimes played to them after a show. During World War I, Broadway supported the soldiers. Theaters were built to raise money for the war. After the war, shows began to deal with social and political issues. Productions increased dramatically.

The Great Depression hit in the 1930s. The number of productions fell. However, this was a creative time for writers. Interesting shows were written about the state of affairs in the US. Broadway always responded to changes in society. Mass media was too hard to compete with. Nonetheless, Broadway is still an important aspect of American culture.

Page 130

Step 1

W: New York is famous for many things. Broadway is just one of them. Broadway shows are popular with people of all ages. Anyone planning a trip to this city should check out the shows in advance. With so many Broadway musicals coming and going, it can be hard to choose which one to see.

One of the longest running musicals on Broadway was *Cats*. It was composed by Andrew Lloyd Webber. The first show was in London. It has been performed all around the world and has been translated into many languages. It is about a tribe of cats. They meet once a year to choose a cat to be reborn. The actors perform so perfectly. They bear great resemblance to real cats.

Another popular production is *The Lion King*. It is based on a Disney animated film. The musical tells the story of Simba, who is a lion. His father, Mufasa, is the Lion King. Simba will become king in the future. The story is about jealousy and evil. Mufasa dies while still in his prime, and Simba becomes king. Musicals often use animals as the characters. The stories are very entertaining. Usually, the stories are about social issues. The animals represent certain people in politics or the media at that time.

The theater plays an important role in people's lives. Writers have the chance to express their views in a fun way. Sometimes the writers are lucky, and their stories are told all around the world.

[Review 2]

Integrated 1

Page 134

Step 2

M: Before the nineteenth century, very little Russian literature was read worldwide. In the 1830s Russian literature underwent a radical change. It began with the poet Alexander Pushkin. It resulted in two of the most predominant novelists in world literature. They are Leo Tolstoy and Fyodor Dostoevsky.

Russian literature is synonymous with suffering. Dostoevsky has been acknowledged for his use of suffering in his books. *Crime and Punishment* is a good example. This is about a poor student who is resentful of an evil pawn broker. He plots to kill her for her money. He believes that he is doing a good act by killing her. He uses her money to resolve others financial problems. He helps a girl who struggles to support her family after her parent's death. He falls in love with the girl and confesses his crime to her. She encourages him to confess to the police. He is sent to prison, and she follows him and lives in the same city.

The story is not really about his punishment. It is more about his guilt and how it affects him. He confesses to the murder towards the end of the story. He believes it will put an end to his feelings of solitude.

In this story, the writer frequently deals with issues of modern concern. Murder, guilt, love, and religion are common themes in this book. *Crime and Punishment* has been translated into many languages. It has also been made into a movie several times. It is without doubt an intrinsic part of global literature.

Integrated 2

Page 136

Step 1

M: You look very happy. Do you have some good news?

W: I sure do. I had a meeting with the dean today, and he suggested that I should run for student president.

M: Congratulations, but how will you be able to concentrate on your studies and run for president?

W: It will be challenging for sure, but all students deviate from their studies at some stage. It's important to be involved in activities other than study.

M: But study should be your number one priority. You will need to modify your schedule a lot to be able to study and run for president.

W: I'm not obliged to run for it yet. The dean said that I am ambitious and would make a good president. I think I can cater well to the students needs, but I know that my own work can not suffer because of it.

M: I think you would make an excellent president, and there are definitely advantages to it. It will look great on your resume, and you will meet lots of exquisite people.

W: That's true. I've heard that there is usually good camaraderie among the candidates, but that's not a good enough reason to run for president.

M: Why would you like to be president?

W: I think I can resolve some major issues for students. On-campus facilities are subordinate to most other universities.

M: It will take a lot of time and effort to resolve that issue.

W: I know, and I need to decide if it would be better to concentrate on my own work. Good grades are critical to getting a good job, and I don't plan on a career in politics.

Answer Key

[Unit 1]

Independent

Page 7

B

1. I saw it <u>on TV</u>.
2. The gadget <u>allowed you to cut vegetables in stylish ways</u>.
3. The gadget <u>looked like it wasn't useful</u> because <u>I never want to cut my vegetables in stylish ways</u>.

Page 8

A

1. The most expensive gadget that we own is our DVD player.
2. The most useful gadget that we have is our electronic can opener.
3. The most disappointing gadget was the steam cleaner that was supposed to clean floors.
4. Our family really needs to get one of the little robots that always goes around cleaning the floors.

B

Handy	Useless	Easily broken
Useful	Cheap	Not as good as I thought
Suitable	Expensive	Better than I thought

C

What?	My gadget would <u>write down exactly what I am saying</u>.
Why?	I would create this gadget so <u>I wouldn't have to type anymore</u>.
Who?	I think <u>all people, especially secretaries</u>, would buy this.
Why?	This gadget would be useful because <u>it is much easier to talk than it is to type</u>.

D

Organize lots of information
Do tedious chores
Help you to complete things much quicker
Give you more free time
Let you do things you can't normally do

Page 9

F

Sample response 1

Cell phone

Reason 1
- Has many handy features
- Helps to organize life
- Daily planner is really useful
- Lets me stay up-to-date

Reason 2
- Stay in contact with friends
- Can text, email, or call
- Lots of options for communication

Conclusion: I love my cell phone.

Sample response 2

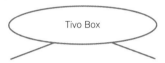

Tivo Box

Reason 1
- Lets me easily record shows
- Never miss my favorite shows
- Can watch when it is suitable for me

Reason 2
- Can fast forward through commercials
- Can save time without watching tedious commercials

Conclusion: A Tivo Box is my favorite gadget.

G

1. up-to-date 2. gadgets 3. irritate
4. tedious 5. commercials

Page 10

Step 2

Sample response 1

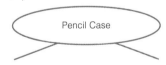

Pencil Case

Reason 1
- Very suitable
- Has all the handy features
- Makes sure I have all the things I need

Reason 2
- Small
- Can easily put it in a bag
- Isn't irritating
- Can put it in my pocket

Conclusion: I love my pencil case.

Step 3

My favorite gadget is <u>my old pencil case</u>. It has <u>all kinds of handy features like a place for my pencils, erasers, and a built-in pencil sharpener. It is not up-to-date, and it isn't particularly fancy, but it is very suitable for me. This makes sure that I always have the things that I need</u>. But most importantly, <u>it is small. I can easily fit it into my bag and it never irritates me. It is really light, and sometimes I can even put it in my pocket</u>. I love my <u>pencil case</u>.

Step 2

Sample response 2

Reason 1
- Can read when others want to sleep
- Doesn't irritate others

Reason 2
- Can read before going to bed
- Irritates me to get out of bed to turn off light

Conclusion: I love my reading light.

Step 3

My favorite gadget is <u>my small reading light</u>. It has <u>a small light and a clip that I can use to attach the light to my book. It is great because I can read at night when other people around me want to sleep.</u> But most importantly, <u>I can read before I go to bed. It irritates me to get out of bed right before I fall asleep</u> to turn off the lights. My small light lets me <u>stay in bed</u>. I love my <u>reading light</u>.

Integrated

Page 11

B
1. The university will <u>close the campus hospital</u>.
2. It is closing it in order to <u>build a new library</u>.
3. I think the conversation will be about <u>the bad results of closing the hospital</u>.

Page 12

B

Man	Woman
• Saw <u>a notice at the hospital</u>	• Didn't <u>see the notice</u>
• The university <u>wants to close the campus hospital</u>	• The current <u>library is too small</u>
• They want <u>to build a new library</u>	• A new one would <u>be wonderful</u>
• The hospital is <u>very important</u>	• Could go to <u>another hospital</u>
• This one is <u>convenient</u>	• Some are <u>near the university</u>
• Lives <u>in the dorms</u>	• Lives <u>in a house in the city</u>
• Doesn't have <u>a car</u>	• Will <u>go to the meeting with the man</u>
• Doesn't want to <u>ride the bus sick</u>	
• Is <u>furious</u>	
• Going to <u>the meeting</u>	

Page 13

D

The conversation is about closing the campus hospital so that <u>they can use the money to build a new library</u>.
A. The man is very <u>angry about the university closing the campus hospital</u>.

B. The hospital is
  1. very <u>important</u>
  2. <u>convenient</u> for students living in the dorms
C. Students will be <u>healthier if they have access to a physician</u>
D. He had to <u>go to the hospital last week</u>
E. He can't go to another hospital because
  1. he doesn't <u>have a car</u>
  2. he doesn't want <u>to take the bus when he is sick</u>
E. He will go <u>to the meeting</u>

F
1. physician
2. facilities
3. recover
4. diagnosis
5. treatments

Page 14
Step 2

Man	Woman
• Got a copy <u>of the new medical center charges</u>	• Didn't <u>know about the changes</u>
• The university <u>didn't get enough money from the government</u>	• Thought the <u>medical center was free</u>
• Students will have to <u>pay to see a doctor and pay more for medicine and treatment</u>	• Went <u>there last week</u>
	• Has some <u>medicine</u>
• Most students <u>will be unhappy</u>	• But <u>has to buy some more</u>
• Many people will <u>get sick</u>	• Thinks there is <u>another way to get money</u>
• Maybe the university will <u>take away the charges</u>	• Thinks some <u>students will avoid going to the doctor</u>
	• Is going to <u>complain</u>

Page 15
Step 4

The conversation is about the medical center now charging to see a doctor and <u>for medication</u>.
A. The woman is <u>unhappy</u>
B. She went there last week
  1. Got <u>medication</u>
  2. Needs <u>more medication but can't afford it</u>
C. The other students will be <u>unhappy</u>
  1. They may avoid <u>going to the doctor</u>
  2. They may get <u>sick</u>
D. There must be another <u>way to find the money for the medical center</u>
  1. She will <u>complain</u>
  2. She hopes the university will <u>take away the charges</u>

Step 5

The conversation is about <u>the medical center now charging to see a doctor and for medication</u>. The woman is <u>unhappy about the changes</u>. She went there <u>last week and got some medicine</u>.

However, she needs more medicine, and she can't afford to pay more. She is sure the other students will be unhappy and they may avoid going to the doctor. As a result, many people may get sick. She thinks that there must be another way to find the money for the medical center, so she is going to complain and maybe the university will take away the charges.

Check-up

Page 16

1. daily planner   2. current   3. particularly
4. student union   5. fast forward   6. suitable
7. fever   8. Medicine
9. handy   10. furious

[Unit 2]

Independent

Page 17

B
1. I usually go to McDonald's for fast food.
2. I eat fast food about once a week.
3. After eating fast food, I feel full, and sometimes I even feel a little bit sick.

Page 18

A
1. I can exercise to make my body healthier.
2. I drink too much coffee, which is bad for my body.
3. I want to lose a little bit of weight to make my body healthier.
4. I think I am pretty healthy. I exercise, but I am a little bit fat, and I drink too much coffee.

B

Eat lots of vegetables   Smoke
Work out
Eat foods with lots of preservatives
Get lots of sleep
Go hiking or running   Stay up all night to study

C

What?	I can try to drink less soda and eat less meat.
How?	I will do this by eating at home more often.
When?	I will start doing this at the end of the school year because I am very busy now.
Why?	I want to do this because it will make me lose weight and feel better.

D

Convenient	Delicious	Lots of preservatives
Unhealthy	Quick	Always available
Easy to eat	Cheap	Always tastes the same

Page 19

F
Sample response 1

Doesn't lead to worse health

Reason 1
- Lifestyle is more important
- People who eat fast food tend to have an unhealthy lifestyle
- Usually don't exercise

Reason 2
- Some are healthy who eat fast food
- Brother is slim and muscular and eats fast food
- He works out and is very healthy

Conclusion: Eating fast food doesn't always make your health worse.

Sample response 2

Does lead to worse health

Reason 1
- No nutritional value
- Loaded with fat, salt and other preservatives
- These things make us fat and unhealthy

Reason 2
- Always available
- Healthy cheap food not available
- People are forced to eat unhealthy food

Conclusion: I think fast food is the main cause of our worsening health.

G
1. force   2. muscular   3. determining
4. preservatives   5. nutritional

Page 20

Sample response 1
Step 2

Fast food makes us unhealthy

Reason 1
- Fast food is everywhere
- Children see fast food commercials
- Parents are forced to give fast food to kids

Reason 2
- Difficult to determine how healthy food is
- Think eating it is a little bit unhealthy but it is very unhealthy

Conclusion: Eating fast food is dangerous for our health.

Step 3

I think that fast food has caused our worsening health. I think this because fast food is everywhere. Children see commercials on TV for fast food and they want it. The parents are then forced to give their children food with no nutritional value. In addition, fast food restaurants make it difficult to determine how healthy their food is. People are particularly surprised when they learn how much fat is in a Big Mac at McDonald's. People think they are eating something a little bit unhealthy, but they are eating something that is incredibly fattening. Eating fast food is dangerous for our health.

Sample response 1
Step 2

Reason 1
- Lots of food at the supermarket is unhealthy
- People still eat unhealthy food

Reason 2
- Fast food restaurants offer healthy food as well
- Can order a salad
- Not forced to eat hamburgers

Conclusion: Eating fast food doesn't have a relationship to our worsening health.

Step 3

I think that fast food has no effect on our worsening health. I think this because there are lots of foods that are sold at the supermarket that are loaded with fats and preservatives. People still eat a lot of these foods. No one is complaining that the supermarket is making people unhealthy. In addition, fast food restaurants offer healthy food as well. You can order a salad at almost any fast food restaurant now. You are not forced to eat a hamburger and French fries. Eating fast food doesn't have a relationship to our worsening health.

Integrated

Page 21
B
1. Roman and Greek sculptures were made from bronze and marble.
2. Sculptures were made to show the greatness of a man or an event.
3. I think this lecture will be about how Greeks and Romans made sculptures.

Page 22
B
Beauty
- Greek and Roman sculptures are very ornate and elaborate
- People travel to see the beautifully preserved sculptures

Style
- Greek and Roman sculptures are very similar
- This is because the Romans copied the Greek style

Reasons they were made
- Made to tell stories about famous wars or events
- Statues were made to honor great men

Materials
- Made from bronze and marble
- Romans preferred bronze statues

Page 23
D
The lecture and passage were about Ancient Greek and Roman sculptures.
A. Sculptures
   1. They are beautiful and ornate
   2. They are very similar
B. How it was learned
   1. Greeks started it
   2. Romans learned through trade and war
C. Uses
   1. Stories of an important war or event
   2. Statues honored important people
D. Materials
   1. Bronze stronger
   2. Marble more easily sculpted, more realistic
Conclusion: Greek and Roman sculptures are great.

F
1. dominates   2. renowned   3. intricate
4. preserve   5. ornate

Page 24
Step 2

Bronze
- Bronze is an important metal
- It is a combination of tin and copper
- Bronze is both light and strong
- It was used in both war and in sculptures
- During wars they were melted down and made into weapons

Marble
- Marble is soft and weak
- A thin piece can easily break
- A good example of this is the *Venus Di Milo*
- Feet and legs are often thicker than a normal person's
- Marble is taken from the ground in large blocks

Answer Key

Page 25

Step 4

The passage and lecture were about <u>how bronze and marble sculptures are different</u>.

A. Bronze
1. It is good for <u>sculptures and to make weapons with</u>
2. It is very <u>strong and light</u>
3. During wars <u>it was melted down and turned into weapons</u>
4. There aren't many bronze statues because <u>there were many wars and they needed the bronze</u>

B. Marble
1. Marble is <u>beautiful, but it is also weak</u>
2. The problem with marble is <u>that it breaks easily</u>
3. Examples of problems with marble are <u>arms breaking off the *Venus Di Milo* and heads falling off statues</u>
4. Marble statues often have <u>thicker legs and feet to help support the weight</u>

Step 5

The passage and lecture were about <u>how bronze and marble are used to make sculptures</u>. Bronze is good for <u>making weapons as well as making sculptures</u>. It is good because <u>it is both light and strong. This allows the sculptor to make different designs</u>. During wars, <u>bronze statues were melted down and turned into weapons such as swords, knives, and arrows</u>. Marble is <u>very beautiful, but it is also very weak</u>. The problem with it is that it <u>breaks very easily at thin points</u>. Examples of marble breaking are <u>the famous sculpture *Venus Di Milo* as well as other statues that seem to have lost their heads</u>. Marble statues often have thicker legs and feet. This is to help support the weight of the statue.

Check-up

Page 26

1. relationship	2. honor	3. slim
4. bronze	5. worsen	6. loaded
7. sculpt	8. skilled	
9. work out	10. marble	

[Unit 3]

Independent

Page 27

B
1. I had to decide <u>what to eat for lunch</u>.
2. I wasn't happy with my decision because <u>I didn't like the sandwich that I chose</u>.
3. I feel that <u>this wasn't an important decision</u>.

Page 28

A
1. I will have to decide which company I want to work for.
2. This is important because I want to work at the same company for a long time.
3. I will have to decide which person I want to marry.
4. This is important because I want to have a family, and I want to be sure that I have the right spouse to start a family with.

B

Getting married
Choosing a job
Finding an ideal place to live
Meeting new friends
Buying a house
Starting a family
Choosing how to spend your money
Where to go on vacation

C

What?	I had to decide <u>whether or not to accept a new job</u>.
When?	This happened <u>a couple of weeks ago</u>.
What happened?	The result of the decision was that <u>I decided not to take the job</u>.
Why?	I decided this because <u>I didn't feel that the job was right for me</u>.

D

Rich	Challenged	Enthusiastic
Laid back	Intense	Peaceful
Energetic	Relaxed	Inspired

Page 29

F

Sample response 1

College Major

Reason 1
- Often leads to a career later
- You will use this for next 30 years
- Wrong decision can make you miserable for a long time

Reason 2
- Must be passionate about it
- Must be energetic and excited to work

Conclusion: Choosing a major is the most important decision you can make.

Sample response 2

Where you live

Reason 1
- Imperative to find a city that matches personality
- Cosmopolitan people won't like rural areas
- Rural people might not like cities

Reason 2
- City can attract other people with similar personality interests
- Makes it easier to make friends

Conclusion: Choosing an ideal place to live is the most important decision a person can make.

G

1. cosmopolitan   2. ideal   3. captivates
4. imperative   5. energetic

Page 30

Step 2

Sample response 1

A spouse

Reason 1
- Will have to make us happy for the rest of life.
- If bored, and gloomy, will be unhappy for long time

Reason 2
- Help raise children
- Should be energetic and helpful
- Will help to be sure children are smart and healthy

Conclusion: Choosing the right spouse is the most important decision we make.

Step 3

The most important decision that we have to make is <u>who we choose to be our husband or wife</u>. This is so important because <u>this person will have to make us happy for the rest of our lives. If we are bored, gloomy, or dissatisfied with our spouse, we will be unhappy for a really long time</u>. It is also important to <u>choose a good spouse because that person will also help you to raise children. An ideal spouse will be energetic and helpful. This will ensure that your children grow up smart, responsible and healthy</u>. Choosing the right <u>spouse</u> is the most important decision that we have to make.

Step 2

Sample response 2

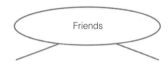

Friends

Reason 1
- Friends shape who we are
- Share interests, attitudes, and beliefs

Reason 2
- Friends captivate us
- Lead us to do things we don't do
- This can be good and bad

Conclusion: Choosing the right friends is the most important decision we make.

Step 3

The most important decision that we make is <u>who we are friends with</u>. This is so important because <u>our friends shape who we are. We tend to share similar beliefs, attitudes, and values as our friends</u>. It is also important to <u>choose good friends because our friends captivate us. Friendship can lead us to do things we don't normally do. This can be both a good and a bad thing. It's important to have friends who make us do good things</u>. Choosing the right <u>friends</u> is the most important decision we make.

Integrated

Page 31

B

1. The students are discussing <u>if Lisa should postpone her exam or not</u>.
2. Her grandmother <u>is sick and will need an operation urgently. She is worried that she will be too distracted to do well in her exams</u>.
3. I think the rest of the conversation will be about <u>why she should postpone her exams</u>.
4. I think the student should <u>postpone the exam</u>.

Answer Key

A

Woman	Man
• Grandmother is ill but has exam • Doesn't know if she should postpone exam • Has breathing disorder and needs operation • Studying hard but might be distracted • Has a strong bond with her grandmother • Took care of her so she should be there for her grandmother • Already studied so should be easy to do later • Said they would grant a deferral • Hard decision to make	• Thinks Lisa looks stressed • Won't grandmother be unconscious and unaware of her being there • Maybe she should take the exam • Shouldn't exert too much pressure on herself • Asks if she is sure the institute will grant a deferral • Seems too upset to do the exam • Can't do anything for her anyway

B

1. The students discuss how the grandmother's illness will distract the girl from doing well in her exam.
2. The student's reasons for doing the exam are that her grandmother will be unconscious and will not know if she is there or not.

D

The conversation is about if the student should postpone her exams or do them now.
A. Reasons for postponing the exam
   1. Grandmother needs an operation and the student feels that she should be there with her
   2. Too distracted to do well in her exam
   3. Will be easy to study again as she already has the knowledge
B. Reasons for doing the exam now
   1. Has studied hard and is prepared
   2. Grandmother will be unconscious and can't do anything for her anyway
   3. Postponing the exam will exert a lot of pressure on the student
Conclusion: I think the student should postpone the exam because she is too upset to do well now.

E

Conclusion: I think the student should do the exam now because she is prepared for it, and her grandmother will not know if she is there or not because she will be unconscious.

G

1. grant   2. bond   3. institute
4. deny   5. postpone

Step 1

Woman	Man
• Has a sleeping disorder, and it has been really bad recently • Requested a deferral but is not sure that she should postpone the exams • Exerts too much pressure on herself at exam time • Collapsed and was unconscious last week • Always had the disorder and doesn't know if she will perform any better later • Hopes the medicine will help her relax and concentrate	• Should postpone exams for a while • Medicine will help her relax and she will be more prepared in a few months • Let the institute decide

Step 3

The conversation is about the student's disorder and if she should defer her exams.
A. Reasons for deferral
   1. Student has a sleeping disorder and it has been really bad lately
   2. Medicine will help her relax and concentrate
   3. Break from studying may be good for her right now
B. She collapsed last week and was unconscious for a couple of minutes.
C. Should do the exam now because
   1. she always had the disorder and not sure that she will perform any better later
   2. she has studied hard all semester and attended all of her classes
   3. maybe she should do the exam and get it over with
Conclusion: I would postpone the exams until my condition had improved.

Step 4

The conversation is about postponing exams because of a sleeping disorder. The student has been feeling very bad recently and was even unconscious because of it. If she defers, the medicine might help her relax so that she can perform better later. She also thinks that maybe a break from studying will be good for her right now. She is not sure what to do because she has always had the disorder. She has studied hard and thinks that maybe she should do the exam now and get it over with. I would try to defer the exam and hope that the medicine would help me to relax and concentrate on my studies so that I would do better in the exams at a later date.

Page 36

1. deferral   2. leads   3. stressed
4. rural   5. disorder   6. unconscious
7. miserable   8. exert
9. dissatisfied 10. gloomy

[Unit 4]

Independent

Page 37

B

1. I have a lot of knowledge <u>about fashion</u>.
2. I got this knowledge by <u>reading fashion magazines and going shopping often</u>.
3. I will continue to learn about this by <u>designing my own clothes</u>.

Page 38

A

1. I am an experienced fisherman.
2. I have been fishing for over fifteen years.
3. I have learned to be patient and to not get angry when I can't control something.
4. My experience has taught me to be more patient. This lets me enjoy fishing more.

B

Drawing
Playing computer games
Studying for tests
Sports
Playing music
Fixing computers
Dating
Going through trying family situations

C

What?	I am good at <u>taking tests</u>.
How?	I became good by <u>studying hard and developing test taking strategies</u>.
Why?	I am good at this because <u>I usually get really high scores on my tests</u>.
How?	I will continue to improve by <u>studying hard and making new test strategies</u>.

D

Smart	Hard working	Old	Learning
Rigors	Succeed	Trying	Accomplish
Calm			

Page 39

F

Sample response 1

Experience more important than knowledge

Reasons
- Anyone can read books
- Not everyone has been through trying things
- Experience proves you can succeed even when things don't go well

Examples
- As a student preferred experienced teachers
- Always were in control
- Knew how to teach something best

Conclusion: I would much rather be experienced than knowledgeable.

Sample response 2

Experience and knowledge both important

Reasons
- They go hand in hand
- Experience without knowledge will be unsuccessful
- Knowledge without experience leads to failure

Examples
- Grandma is wise and experienced but won't ask her for computer help
- College graduates have lots of knowledge
- But they find it difficult to adjust to life at work

Conclusion: Experience and knowledge are both very important.

G

1. rigors   2. trying   3. knowledge
4. extraordinarily 5. necessarily

Page 40

Step 2

Sample response 1

Knowledge more important than experience

Reasons
- Knowledge always up-to-date
- Knowledge can be used on different things
- Experience cannot be used so generally

Examples
- Needed in modern business world
- Old companies like GM suffering
- Have lots of experience, but do not have up-to-date knowledge in car industry

Conclusion: Knowledge is far more important than experience.

Step 3

I think that <u>knowledge is more important than experience</u>. I think this because <u>knowledge is always up-to-date. If you have a lot of knowledge you can always succeed. Knowledge can also be used on a variety of different matters. Experience cannot always be used so generally.</u> An example of this is <u>in business today. Many old companies like GM are going through very trying times now. They have a lot of experience, but they do not have the up-to-date knowledge to succeed in the modern car industry. Knowledge</u> is far more important than <u>experience</u>.

Step 2

Sample response 2

Experience more important than knowledge

Reasons
- Experience is knowledge in real life
- Knowledge without experience is useless
- Experience lets us make good decisions without knowing a situation

Examples
- Experienced traveler
- Can communicate with locals without knowing the language
- Experience taught him to communicate without talking

Conclusion: Experience is far more important than knowledge.

Step 3

I think that <u>experience is more important than knowledge</u>. I think this because <u>experience is knowledge that is used in real life. Knowledge without the experience to go with it is useless. Experience also allows us to make good decisions in new situations without necessarily having the knowledge about the situation.</u> An example of this is <u>an experienced traveler knows how to communicate with locals in a foreign country without having the knowledge of their language. His real life experiences taught him to communicate without speaking.</u> Experience is far more important than <u>knowledge</u>.

Integrated

Page 41
B
1. The lecture is mainly about <u>the brain</u>.
2. The brain produces <u>our thoughts, actions, memories, feelings, and experiences</u>.
3. I think the professor <u>will talk about how the brain functions</u>.

Page 42
A
- The brain produces <u>our thoughts, actions, memories, feelings, and experiences</u>
- Brains form <u>connections, which store memories and habits and shape personalities</u>
- Patterns change and <u>no two brains are alike</u>
- Human brain <u>consists of three parts</u>
- The first <u>segment is in the lower section and is called the brain stem</u>
- Controls <u>instincts, reflexes, physical functioning, and tells us when to eat and drink</u>
- The second <u>is called the mid-brain and lies above the brain stem</u>
- Allows us <u>to sense pain and pleasure, stores patterns of movement, and repeated tasks</u>
- The third <u>is called the neocortex and allows us to think, set goals, and solve problems</u>
- Second and third <u>sections must work together for maturing into adulthood</u>

B
1. The professor talks about <u>three sections of the brain</u>.
2. The professor says <u>the second and third parts must work together for maturing into</u> adulthood.

Page 43
D
The lecture is about <u>the brain</u>.
A. The brain
   1. Produces <u>every thought, action, memory, feeling, and experience</u>
   2. Forms <u>connections which store memories, habits, and shapes personalities</u>
   3. Connections <u>change constantly and no two brains are alike</u>
B. The human brain <u>has three segments</u>
   1. Brain stem <u>controls instincts, reflexes, and basic functioning</u>
   2. Mid-brain <u>allows us to sense pleasure and pain</u>
   3. Neocortex <u>allows us to think, set goals, and solve problems</u>
Conclusion: The brain <u>is complex and is responsible for thoughts, feelings, and actions</u>.

F
1. reflexes   2. connection   3. functioning
4. Harmony   5. maturing

Page 44
Step 1
- Concussions are <u>very common</u>
- They are <u>the least serious form of brain injury</u>

- Brain injury is commonly caused through sports injuries
- Symptoms include dizziness, nausea, loss of memory, and loss of consciousness
- Sometimes, players return to game when they shouldn't
- Recovery time depends on how severe the injury is
- Diagnosing is usually straightforward
- Doctor will ask questions and check reflexes
- If serious, brain scan is performed

Step 3

The lecture is about concussions.
A. Least serious brain injury
   1. Brain is made up of soft tissue and is cushioned by spinal fluid
   2. Brain receives an injury when it gets tossed around and bangs off the skull
B. Causes and symptoms
   1. Commonly caused through sports injuries
   2. Symptoms include dizziness, nausea, loss of memory, and sometimes loss of consciousness
C. Doctors ask questions, check reflexes, and do a brain scan.
D. Recovery time depends on how severe the injury is
Conclusion: Concussions are the least serious head injury but symptoms are not always obvious.

Page 45
Step 4

The lecture is about concussions. Concussions are very common and are the least serious form of brain injury. The brain is made up of soft tissue, cushioned by spinal fluid. Brain injury is caused when the brain gets tossed around and bangs off the skull. Concussions occur commonly through sports injuries. The symptoms include dizziness, nausea, loss of memory, and sometimes loss of consciousness. Concussions are diagnosed by asking questions, testing reflexes, and brain scans. They are very easy to diagnose. The recovery time depends on how severe the injury is. They are the least serious head injury but symptoms are not always obvious.

Check-up

Page 46

1. Organ
2. failure
3. nerve
4. matters
5. Neurons
6. brain stem
7. bursting
8. cells
9. hand-in-hand
10. succeed

[Unit 5]

Independent

Page 47
B
1. My hobby is playing the saxophone in a band.
2. I spend almost thirty hours a week practicing with my band.
3. I do my hobby in an old building near my friend's house. We can be really loud there.

Page 48
A
1. I like going to the art galleries downtown.
2. I like going there because I get to see all sorts of new modern art by young artists.
3. I try to go every week, but it is usually more like once every two weeks.
4. I wish I could go more often because I want to be an artist when I get older. Going to the galleries can help me to learn new skills and techniques.

B
Museum
Sporting events
Downtown
Bookstore
Friend's home
Park
Library
Coffee shop
Restaurants
Gym
Soccer field
River/lake

C

Where?	I have to go to extra classes after school.
How often?	I go there every day. I even have to go on Saturdays.
What?	When I'm there, I have to study for my college entrance exams.
Why?	I have to go to after-school classes because I want to get into a really good university.

D
Studying
Discussing stuff in the news
Chatting with friends
Shopping
Getting dressed in the morning
Playing video games
Watching movies
Visiting family
Going to school

Answer Key

Page 49
F
Sample response 1

Movie Theater

Reason 1
- Love watching innovative special effects
- Love seeing incredible explosions
- See how effects have improved

Reason 2
- Hang out with classmates
- Talk and see a movie
- Go for coffee and criticize or compliment the movie

Conclusion: I love going to the movie theater.

Sample response 2

Nursing Home

Reason 1
- Visit my grandma
- Hard for her to leave the home
- Have a lot in common
- Always discuss politics and articles in newspaper

Reason 2
- Volunteer on weekends
- People there have family far away
- They are lonely
- Want to talk to people

Conclusion: I enjoy it and I think it makes them feel better.

G
1. compliment   2. articles   3. incredible
4. innovative   5. visit

Page 50
Step 2
Sample response 1

The park

Reason 1
- Love playing basketball with friends
- Can discuss things
- Visit with friends

Reason 2
- Can play against incredible players
- Can improve basketball skills
- Feels great when good players give a compliment

Conclusion: I spend a lot of time at the park.

Step 3

   I often go to <u>the park to play basketball</u>. I go there because <u>I love playing basketball with my friends. We can discuss things, visit with each other, and then go and run around and play</u>. Another reason why I go there is because <u>I get a chance to play against some incredible players. By playing with them, I think that I improve my skills. I feel great when one of the really good players gives me a compliment. It feels great</u>. I spend a lot of time at <u>the park</u>.

Step 2
Sample response 2

The office

Reason 1
- Need a part time job
- Want to visit friend in Switzerland
- Mountains are incredible

Reason 2
- Get a job after university
- Company is really innovative
- Can get a good job later

Conclusion: I enjoy it and I think it makes them feel better.

Step 3

   I often go to <u>work at an office</u>. I go there because <u>I need a part time job. I am trying to save enough money so I can go to Switzerland to visit my friend. She tells me the mountains are incredible</u>. Another reason I go there is because <u>I want to get a job after university. My company is really innovative and working at this company will teach me a lot of really important skills that can help me to get a job later</u>. I spend a lot of time at <u>my office</u>.

Integrated

Page 51
B
1. The dorm will <u>change the quiet hours when residents have to be quiet</u>.
2. They are changing the hours because <u>the residents are unhappy with the current "quiet hours."</u>
3. I think the conversation will be about <u>how the students feel about the new quiet hours</u>.

Page 52
B

Man	Woman
• Is having <u>a party</u> • Didn't know <u>about the changes to the "quiet hours"</u> • Thinks it will <u>be difficult to be quiet</u> • Thinks they should be <u>more flexible on their policy</u>	• Can't <u>go to the party</u> • Has a <u>test</u> • Thinks there are <u>pros and cons to the new hours</u> • Is <u>optimistic</u> • Has trouble <u>studying when there is noise</u> • Other students have <u>jobs and sports</u> • Likes <u>to get a good-night's sleep before work</u> • People need to be <u>aware of others</u> and <u>respectful</u>

Page 53
D
The woman is <u>optimistic about the new "quiet hours."</u>

A. The woman
1. thinks <u>there are pros and cons</u>
2. thinks it will enable <u>a better environment</u>
3. has <u>trouble studying when there is noise</u>
B. She likes <u>to get a good night's sleep before work</u>
C. Students
1. have <u>jobs and sports</u>
   • The woman is happy that <u>the quiet hours happen on the weekend</u>
2. can still have <u>fun</u>
   • Be <u>aware of others</u>
   • Be <u>respectful</u>

F
1. pros and cons   2. enable   3. Flexibility
4. rigid   5. stable

Page 54
Step 2

Woman	Man
• Have been <u>complaints</u> • Guests will <u>have to leave earlier</u> • Some students will <u>complain about the new policy</u> • Thinks it will <u>reduce the number of arguments</u> • There will be <u>no exceptions</u> • Everyone <u>will be treated equally</u>	• Thinks <u>it's a great idea</u> • Had problems with <u>assignments</u> • It's hard <u>to concentrate when there are so many people around</u> • Is <u>happy about the new guest hours</u> • People will <u>be more respectful</u> • Will bring <u>peace to the building</u> • The majority <u>of students will be happier</u>

Page 55
Step 4

The man thinks <u>the changes are a great idea</u>.
A. It gets really <u>noisy</u>
B. He
1. thinks it's hard <u>to concentrate when people are around</u>
2. has had problems with <u>his assignments before</u>
3. is happy <u>about the reduced hours</u>
C. People
1. are going to <u>be more respectful</u>
2. will have fewer <u>arguments</u>
3. will be <u>happy about the changes</u>
D. The building will be <u>more peaceful</u>.

Step 5

The man thinks <u>the changes are a great idea</u>. At the moment it gets <u>really noisy</u>, and he thinks it's hard to <u>concentrate on his university assignments when there are many people around. He has had problems with his assignments before because of</u>

<u>that</u>. Therefore, he is happy <u>that the guest hours have been reduced</u>. He also thinks that people are going to <u>be more respectful of each other so there will be fewer arguments. He thinks that will mean that the majority of the students will be happier and that his building will be more peaceful</u>.

Check-up
Page 56
1. special effects   2. victims   3. nursing home
4. reformed   5. peacefully 6. advise
7. come to life   8. explosion
9. optimistic   10. discuss

[Unit 6]

Independent
Page 57

B
1. I go shopping most often at <u>Target</u>.
2. I go shopping there because <u>it is cheap, and they have both clothes and food</u>.
3. I prefer shopping at <u>big stores</u> because <u>they have a lot of things for me to look at and buy</u>.

Page 58

A
1. My favorite chain restaurant is Outback Steakhouse.
2. This is my favorite chain restaurant because they have the absolute best steaks.
3. My favorite item at Outback Steakhouse is their Baby Back Ribs.
4. I prefer Outback Steakhouse to independent steak restaurants because their steaks are the best tasting steaks I have ever had.

B
Great selection	Too big
Same quality everywhere	Hard to find specialty items
Know what to expect	Doesn't support locals
Often cheaper	
Great bargains	Not very good service

C
What?	They sell <u>pet supplies and other things for pets</u>.
Who?	The owners of the store <u>live down the street from where I live</u>.
Why?	I would shop there because <u>the owners are really nice, and they always take really good care of my dog</u>.

Answer Key

Where? The store is located <u>right around the corner from my home</u>.

D
Friendly
Stylish
Smaller
Great service
Limited/smaller selection
More expensive
Treat employees better
Wisely operated
Harder to find
Few locations

Page 59

F

Sample response 1

Independent Stores

Reason 1
- Supporting your own community
- Money stays in your community

Reason 2
- Helping people at store
- Help to pay their salary
- Increase their standard of living
- Chain stores pay lower salaries

Conclusion: Shopping at independent stores helps to make your community stronger. This is because you are directly helping people in your community more.

Sample response 2

It doesn't matter where you shop

Reason 1
- Choose place with best bargains
- Everyone works hard for his or her money
- Should spend money wisely

Reason 2
- Shop where you get a good deal
- Every store competes for business

Conclusion: In the end, the more money you have in your pocket, the happier you are going to be.

G
1. wisely
2. standard of living
3. chain stores
4. locals
5. hard-earned

Page 60

Step 2

Sample response 1

Chain Stores

Reason 1
- Much bigger
- Lets them offer better deals and bargains
- Lets me keep more money

Reason 2
- Know exactly what to expect
- Same anywhere in the world
- Don't worry about finding things

Conclusion: It is best to shop at chain stores.

Step 3

I think it is better to shop at <u>chain stores</u>. I like to shop at <u>chain stores</u> because <u>they are much bigger. Because they are bigger, they can offer much better deals and bargains. This lets me keep more hard-earned money in my pocket and increase my standard of living</u>. They are also better because <u>they are the same anywhere you go. I know exactly what to expect if I go to a 7-11 in America, Japan, or Europe. I like not having to worry about finding something</u>. It is best to shop at <u>chain stores</u>.

Step 2

Sample response 2

Small Stores

Reason 1
- Don't care independent or chain
- Employees nicer
- Employees knowledgeable and experienced

Reason 2
- People who operate stores are more passionate
- They are the owners
- Usually locals who want successful business
- Make customers happy

Conclusion: It is best to shop at small stores.

Step 3

I think it is better to shop at <u>small stores. I don't care if it is an independent or chain store</u>. I like to shop at <u>small stores</u> because <u>the employees are usually much nicer. They are usually more experienced and knowledgeable about their store</u>. They are also better because <u>the people who operate the stores are usually more passionate about their stores. This is because they are the owners. They usually are locals who want to have a successful business. They will work hard to make sure the customers are happy</u>. It is best to shop at <u>small stores</u>.

Page 61

B

1. They have to flee because <u>there is fighting and they need to save their lives</u>.
2. They face problems with <u>learning new languages, new currencies, customs, and adjusting to a new way of life</u>.
3. I think this lecture will be about <u>how refugees adapt to their new homeland</u>.

Page 62

B

Leaving

- Their governments <u>are corrupt and at war</u>
- There isn't enough <u>food</u>
- They are often <u>minorities who feel they must leave or be killed</u>

Problems

- They cannot <u>communicate with the locals</u>
  - They overcome this by <u>taking intensive classes</u>
  - They have to <u>study very hard</u>
- The weather <u>is very different to their homelands</u>

Organizations/other refugees

- They help to <u>find jobs</u>
- They help adjust <u>to new problems and variables in their new land</u>

In the end

- They learn to <u>drive, shop at the supermarket, and root for the local sports teams</u>

Page 63

D

The lecture and the passage were about <u>how African refugees adjust to life in a new homeland</u>.
A. They leave because
   1. their governments are <u>corrupt and at war</u>
   2. their homelands don't have <u>enough food</u>
   3. they are worried that <u>they will be killed</u>
B. The problems they face are
   1. they often cannot <u>communicate</u>
   2. the weather is <u>a big change</u>
C. Help
   1. <u>Other refugees and organizations</u> help refugees adjust
   2. They get help <u>finding jobs</u>
   3. They teach them useful things like <u>driving a car and shopping at a store</u>

F

1. minority   2. currency   3. regime
4. variables   5. inherent

Page 64

Step 2

How it started

- In Iraq, the regime was <u>corrupt and evil</u>
- Regime was defeated but <u>fighting continued</u>
- This made people <u>leave their homeland</u>

Where they went

- They went to <u>neighboring countries</u>
- They come with their own <u>customs such as language, food, and religion</u>

What they do

- They make <u>their new homes comfortable</u>
- They start <u>mosques and restaurants</u>
- This is so <u>they can pray, eat, and communicate easily with others</u>

Theater

- Iraqis have <u>a long history in the theater</u>
- Plays show <u>problems inherent in all their lives</u>
- Plays are <u>funny at first but surprising and sad at the end</u>
- Enjoy them because <u>they share many of the same feelings</u>

Page 65

Step 4

This passage and lecture were about <u>Iraqi refugees</u>.
A. The Iraqi regime was <u>corrupt and evil</u>
   1. The regime was defeated but <u>fighting continued</u>
   2. This led to <u>millions of people leaving</u>
B. Iraqis went to <u>neighboring countries</u>
C. They made <u>their new countries more comfortable</u>
   1. They started <u>their own mosques, restaurants</u>
   2. They felt more comfortable because <u>they could be together and communicate easily</u>
D. The theater
   1. Iraqis have a long <u>history in the theater</u>
   2. They write <u>plays that show the problems inherent in their lives</u>
   3. The plays are <u>funny and surprising and usually sad at the end</u>
   4. Iraqi people <u>enjoy them because they share the same feelings</u>

Step 5

This passage and lecture were about <u>Iraqi refugees</u>. The Iraqi regime <u>was corrupt and evil. After the regime was defeated fighting continued</u>. Iraqis left to <u>neighboring countries</u>. They made their lives <u>more comfortable</u>. They did this by <u>starting mosques, restaurants, and other places</u>.

Iraqis go there to communicate easily. Iraqis also love the theater. The plays are usually funny. They are funny, but usually surprising and sad at the end. Iraqis love the theater because they share many of the same feelings as the play shows.

Check-up

Page 66

1. pocket
2. rooting
3. operate
4. Employees
5. Corrupt
6. homeland
7. intensive
8. bargains
9. deal
10. Fortunately

[Review 1]

Independent 1

Page 67
Step 2
Sample response 1

Reason 1
- He is rich
- He has a lot of neat things at his home
- Up-to-date video games at his home

Reason 2
- He is energetic
- Has lots of interests so we always do interesting things
- We always try new things

Conclusion: My uncle is the most fun because he has enough money to let us do whatever is interesting to us.

Sample response 2

Reason 1
- He is hilarious
- He always tells funny jokes
- Always tells really funny stories

Reason 2
- He is very wise
- Everywhere we go he always gives handy advice
- Loves to share his knowledge

Conclusion: My grandpa is the most fun because I always laugh and I always learn something new when I am with him.

Step 3
Sample response 1
My favorite relative is my <u>uncle</u>. I like being with <u>my uncle</u> because <u>he is rich, and he has an extraordinarily neat home</u>. For example, <u>he has all the up-to-date video game systems, and a giant swimming pool in his back yard</u>. My <u>uncle</u> is also great because <u>he is so energetic. He has so</u>

many interests and so much energy to do them all. When I am with <u>my uncle</u> we always <u>spend all day doing new and exciting things. He enables me to try all sorts of interesting things</u>. My <u>uncle</u> is the most fun because <u>he has enough money to do whatever we think is interesting. It is never boring</u>.

Sample response 2
My favorite relative is my <u>grandpa</u>. I like being with <u>my grandpa</u> because <u>he is hilarious</u>. For example, <u>he always tells funny jokes and really funny stories</u>. My <u>grandpa</u> is also great because <u>he always gives me wise advice. Whenever we go somewhere, my grandpa gives me handy advice about what we are doing</u>. When I am with <u>my grandpa</u>, we always <u>talk. He loves to share his knowledge with me</u>. My <u>grandpa</u> is the most fun because <u>I always laugh and I always learn something new when I am with him</u>.

Integrated 1

Page 68
Step 2

Man	Woman
• He is very <u>excited</u>	• Thinks there are <u>pros and cons</u>
• He will go to <u>Austria to study music</u>	• Should be a <u>reward for hard work</u>
• Was worried that <u>he would never get a chance to go</u>	• Thinks she is in <u>the minority</u>
• Thinks there are only <u>pros to going</u>	• Thought levels <u>were good before</u>
• Going will <u>give great opportunities to gain knowledge</u>	• Is happy <u>for her friend</u>
• School shouldn't <u>deny this opportunity to students</u>	

Page 69
Step 4

The conversation is about <u>the lowering of grades in order to study abroad</u>.
A. The man's opinion is that <u>it is important to have the opportunity to go</u>
 1. Students gain <u>knowledge and experience</u>
 2. Thinks there are <u>only pros to going</u>
 3. Schools shouldn't <u>deny this opportunity to its students</u>
B. He will go to <u>Austria to study music</u>
C. He was worried that <u>he would never get a chance to go study abroad</u>
D. The woman thinks <u>that the levels were good before</u>
 1. Studying abroad <u>should be a reward for hard work</u>
 2. But, she is <u>happy for her friend</u>

Step 5

The conversation is about <u>the lowering of grades in order to study abroad</u>. The man thinks that <u>this is a good idea because it is important for students to have the opportunity to go</u>. He thinks that <u>students will gain valuable knowledge and experience. He thinks there are only pros to going</u>. Schools shouldn't <u>deny this opportunity to students based only on their grades</u>. He will go <u>to Austria to study music in Vienna</u>. He was worried that <u>he would never get the opportunity to go because his grades weren't high enough</u>. The woman thinks <u>that the levels were good before</u>. She thinks that <u>studying abroad should be a reward for years of hard work</u>. But, <u>she is happy for her friend</u>.

Integrated 2

Page 70
Step 1

- Teeth and tongue help with <u>communication</u>
- Proper treatment will <u>ensure you have a healthy mouth</u>
- Nice smile can <u>captivate someone</u>
- Smile can <u>enable the start of a good relationship</u>
- The tongue is <u>very muscular</u>
- Moves around to <u>make speech possible</u>
- Teeth let us make <u>'th' sounds</u>
- Both tongue and teeth <u>control air flow</u>
- Healthy mouth <u>makes it easier to communicate</u>
- Should <u>brush and floss teeth everyday</u>

Step 3

This lecture is about how your mouth, tongue and teeth help you communicate.
A. Smiles
    1. A nice smile can <u>help to start a good relationship</u>
    2. It can also <u>captivate someone</u>
B. The tongue
    1. It is very <u>muscular</u>
    2. It moves around to <u>help make speech possible</u>
    3. Also it <u>helps control air flow</u>
C. Teeth
    1. They help us make <u>many different sounds like 'th'</u>
    2. Like the tongue, they also <u>help control airflow</u>
D. Mouth
    1. A healthy mouth <u>makes it much easier to communicate</u>
    2. It is really important to <u>take care of our mouths and brush and floss our teeth every day</u>

Page 71
Step 4

This lecture is about <u>how your mouth, teeth, and tongue help you to communicate</u>. Your mouth helps you smile. This is important because <u>a nice smile can help to start a new relationship. It can captivate someone</u>. The tongue <u>is very muscular. It is strong and it is always moving around. This helps to make speech possible. It also works to control airflow in and out of the mouth</u>. The teeth <u>help us to make important sounds like 'th.'</u> Like the tongue <u>they also help to control airflow</u>. A healthy mouth <u>makes it much easier to communicate with others</u>. It is important to <u>take good care of our mouths and to brush and floss our teeth every day</u>.

Independent 2

Page 72
Step 2
Sample response 1

For the love

Pros
- Do what you want to do
- Preserve your happiness
- Not irritated at work
- Feel at harmony

Cons
- Money can't buy happiness
- No connection between money and happiness
- Become greedy and selfish

Conclusion: You should work for the love of your job.

Sample response 2

For the money

Pros
- Lots of variables in life
- Life is much more stable
- High standard of living, comfortable
- Money gives more flexibility
- Part of maturing process

Cons
- Most people don't like their jobs
- Things can't provide for family
- Can be difficult to be up to up-to-date with bills

Conclusion: You should work for the money.

Step 3

Sample response 1
It is important to do a job for <u>the love of the job</u>. This is imperative because <u>in life it is important to do what you want to do. Life is short. You shouldn't deny your true passions</u>. In addition, <u>you won't feel irritated at work, and you will feel harmony in your life if you love what you do</u>. Others say it is better to work for <u>the money</u>. I disagree. Doing things for <u>the money can't buy your happiness. You will have a lot of currency,</u>

but you won't be happy. There is no connection between money and happiness. You will become greedy and selfish. You should do work for the love of your job.

Sample response 2

It is important to do a job for the money. This is imperative because there are a lot of variables in life. Having money makes your life much more stable. Your standard of living will be much higher and you will be much more comfortable. In addition, having a lot of money gives you much more flexibility. You can do more things. Working a job to earn money is also part of the maturing process as we become adults. Others say it is better to work for the love of the job. I disagree. Doing things for the love of it is unreasonable. Most people don't like their jobs. Not making money will make things difficult on their families. You will have difficulty being up-to-date on the bills. You should work for the money.

[Unit 7]

Independent

Page 73

B

1. I live in Denver, Colorado.
2. My city is located in the middle of America. It is very close to the Rocky Mountains.
3. My city is famous for its beautiful mountains and incredible skiing.

Page 74

A

1. I am very happy with my hometown's schools. We all get a great education.
2. I love my hometown's weather. We have four beautiful seasons every year.
3. I wish there was more for kids to do in my hometown. We can see movies and play outside, but that is all.
4. I am not so happy about how my hometown looks. Many of the old buildings are old, and the streets need to be fixed.

B

Education
Museums
Number of parks
Crime/danger
Transportation
Smoother traffic
Better Internet connections
Entertainment

C

What?	I would improve the pollution in my hometown.
How?	I would improve the pollution by having people drive their cars less.
Why?	I would improve this because the sky is brown and I am always coughing.
Where?	I would first start these improvements by telling people to use the bus more often.

D

Too crowded
Too many traffic jams
Bad pollution
Dirty water
Too noisy
Not enough schools
Not enough police officers
Bad restaurants
Too expensive

Page 75

F

Sample response 1

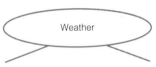

Weather

Reasons
- Limits what I can do
- Like to go outside and be active
- Messes up weekend plans

Examples
- Wanted to go canoeing
- Huge storm so had to stay inside all weekend

Conclusion: The weather in my city often ruins my plans.

Sample response 2

Traffic Jams

Reasons
- Sitting in traffic is dull
- Want city officials to resolve problem

Examples
- Takes one hour to work, should take 20 minutes
- Could leave home early, but have to get up really early
- Perhaps they could make new roads

Conclusion: It looks like I am going to be sitting in traffic everyday for a while.

G

1. modify	2. official	3. smoother
4. resolved	5. priority	

Page 76

Step 2

Sample response 1

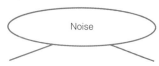

Reasons
- Traffic everywhere
- Cars are loud
- Building new buildings all the time makes a lot of noise

Examples
- Didn't go to sleep until 4 a.m.
- This was due to too much noise

Conclusion: I really wish that the city would do something to resolve the noise here.

Step 3

I dislike the <u>noise</u> of my city. I dislike it because <u>it always seems that there is traffic everywhere. Cars are really loud and they are always making noise. Officials have also made building new buildings a top priority. This has caused a lot of noise at night. For example, last night I didn't go to sleep until 4 a.m. This was because there was too much noise outside of my window and I couldn't fall asleep</u>. I really wish that <u>the city would do something to resolve the noise here</u>.

Step 2

Sample response 2

Reasons
- Makes people angry
- People from other places get treated badly
- Messes up the reputation of the city

Examples
- Saw some foreigners being pushed
- This is horrible

Conclusion: I really wish that people here were nicer to each other.

Step 3

I dislike the <u>rudeness</u> of <u>people in</u> my city. I dislike <u>it because it makes me and other people feel really angry. Everyone always seems to be rude to each other. When people come to my city from other places they get a really bad idea of my city. This messes up the city's reputation. Officials have tried to make people politer, but it hasn't helped. For example, I saw foreigners getting pushed by people as they walked on the street. This is horrible. Changing this attitude needs to be the city's top priority</u>. I really wish that <u>people here were nicer</u>.

Integrated

Page 77

B

1. The students are discussing <u>buying a car to get to university or staying on campus</u>.
2. The student says <u>that his parents are good and that he could still have fun and buy a car</u>.
3. I think the rest of the conversation will be about <u>why he should live on campus</u>.
4. I think the student should <u>live on campus</u>.

Page 78

A

Man	Woman
• Thinking of <u>buying a car and living on parents' estate</u>	• More freedom <u>on campus</u>
• Parents <u>are pretty good</u>	
• They like that <u>older brother lives at home</u>	• Says he seems <u>convinced buying a car and staying home are best</u>
• Doesn't want <u>to deviate from the norm</u>	
• Wants <u>to enjoy university life but too many distractions</u>	
• Being on campus <u>means less travel and selecting his own room</u>	• Thinks it will <u>give him a different scope on being a student</u>
	• He would <u>have to be more independent</u>
• Brother treats him <u>like a subordinate</u>	• Asks <u>about living standards</u>
• Causes <u>tension</u>	
• The living standards on campus are <u>tremendous</u>	

B

1. The students discuss <u>that his parents are good so it's possible to still have fun and buy a car and that distractions on campus may make it difficult to study</u>.
2. The students discuss <u>that it's closer to the university so will not have to travel. The university also has tremendous facilities</u>.

Page 79

D

The conversation is about <u>buying a car to get to university or living on campus</u>.

A. Advantages of buying a car
  1. Could live <u>with parents on their estate</u>
  2. It's intrinsic <u>to study hard and there would be too many distractions living on campus</u>
  3. Will have a <u>car and can drive anywhere</u>
B. Advantages to staying on campus
  1. Closer to <u>university so no travel time</u>
  2. Facilities <u>on campus are tremendous, there is Internet, a gym, and a new library</u>
Conclusion: I think <u>the student should live on campus because there will be no travel time and there are tremendous facilities on campus</u>.

Answer Key

E

Conclusion: I think the student should buy a car to get to university because there are so many distractions on campus and studying hard and succeeding are the most important aspects of being a student.

G

1. subordinates   2. deviate   3. intrinsic
4. estates   5. tension

Page 80
Step 1

Woman	Man
• Can't decide if she should live on campus or buy a car to get to university • Mom is easy going and thinks she should live on campus but dad thinks she should live at home • Great experience but living at home would be cheaper • Tremendous amount of travel time if she lives at home • Doesn't want a part-time job, wants to study hard • Good to get someone else's scope	• Thinks living on campus is an intrinsic part of student life • Campus accommodation has improved greatly • All rooms have wireless Internet and there is also a laundry service • Doesn't have a car so would have to ride the bus • Could use free time to work part-time • Make time for fun

Step 3

The conversation is about the advantages and disadvantages to living at home and living on campus.
A. Advantages and disadvantages to living at home
   1. Would be much cheaper
   2. Standard of living is superior
   3. Take up tremendous amount of travel time
B. Living on campus is an intrinsic part of student life
C. Advantages to living on campus
   1. Has wireless Internet and laundry service
   2. Won't have to ride the bus to university
   3. Get a part-time job
Conclusion: I would prefer to live on campus as it would be more fun and I would like to get a part-time job.

Page 81
Step 4

The conversation is about living at home or on campus while at university. Living at home would be cheaper, the standard of living superior, but it would take up a tremendous amount of the student's time traveling. However, living on campus is an intrinsic part of student life. The university has wireless Internet, so there would be no need to take buses to the university and the student would have more time for a part-time job. I would prefer to live on campus as it would be fun and I would like to get a part-time job.

Page 82

1. scope   2. Canoeing
3. Traffic jams   4. messes up
5. living standards   6. flow
7. tremendous   8. distraction
9. rush-hour   10. select

[Unit 8]

Independent

Page 83

B

1. My favorite food is lasagna.
2. My mom makes this food best.
3. My mom's lasagna is the best because she knows exactly all the things that I like inside it.

Page 84

A

1. I love my mom's cooking because she is a fantastic cook.
2. My mom makes the best cakes and desserts.
3. I eat my mom's cooking every night. I love it.
4. My mom spends at least two hours every day preparing food.

B

Delicious
Filling
Sweet
Original
Creative
Savory
Smells great
Delightful

C

Which?	My favorite restaurant is Sullivan's Steakhouse.
Where?	The restaurant is located downtown near the baseball stadium.
What?	They make steaks, seafood, and an amazing chocolate soufflé.
Why?	I like this restaurant because it has a great atmosphere, and they make the best steaks I have ever eaten.

D

Time consuming
Highly involved
Difficult to cater to everyone's tastes
Hard work
Must clean up after
Children are often picky
Must go to the store to get the food
Can't enjoy the food once you have cooked it

Page 85

F
Sample response 1

Reason 1
- Makes family come together
- Can spend precious time together
- Become intimately involved with others

Reason 2
- Eating out can take a long time
- Can take longer than expected
- Children and adults are busy with other things

Conclusion: I think eating at home is better.

Sample response 2

Reason 1
- It is easier
- No preparation before and after meal
- Restaurant takes care of everything

Reason 2
- Can cater everyone's choices
- Even picky eaters will be happy
- People can eat what they want

Conclusion: Because it is much less of a hassle, I think it is better to go to restaurants for dinner.

G

1. cater   2. involved   3. intimately
4. thereby   5. pursuit

Page 86

Step 2
Sample response 1

Reason 1
- People are busy
- Eating out saves precious time
- Don't have to do chores
- Can do errands on the way to restaurant

Reason 2
- Can go to different restaurants
- Can try different foods
- You can become more involved in food
- Gives a better appreciation of food

Conclusion: I will always eat out when I can.

Sample response 2

Reason 1
- Food makes people happy
- Many are intimately involved in their food
- Have a pursuit of good food

Reason 2
- People who cook cater to their passion for cooking
- They take pride in their food
- They care deeply about it

Conclusion: I will always eat wherever the food is good.

Step 3
Sample response 1

It is better to eat <u>out than it is to eat at home</u>. This is because <u>people are really busy, and eating out saves people's precious time. You don't have to do any chores before you go to eat out. You can even save time by doing some errands on the way to the restaurant.</u> Eating at <u>restaurants</u> is also great because <u>you can go to different restaurants, thereby allowing you to try different foods. This lets you become more involved in food. It gives you a greater appreciation of food.</u> I will always <u>eat out when I can.</u>

Sample response 2

It is better to eat <u>wherever the food tastes good. This is because <u>food makes people really happy. Many people are intimately involved with what they eat. They have a pursuit of good food. It shouldn't matter where you eat as long as the food is good.</u> Eating at <u>places with good food</u> is also great because <u>the chefs at restaurants and family members who do the cooking cater to their own passion for cooking. This makes them take a lot of pride in making really good food. They care deeply about it.</u> I will always <u>eat wherever the food is good.</u>

Integrated

Page 87

B
1. <u>The lecture is mainly about coral.</u>
2. <u>The coral is dying.</u>
3. <u>I think the professor will talk about what is causing the coral to die.</u>

Page 88

A
- Coral is <u>dying more and more often</u>.
- Oceans <u>are becoming warmer and coral bleaching is more widespread</u>.

Answer Key

- Coral depends on algae for food.
- Sea temperatures have been rising for the past one hundred years and are predicted to continue to rise.
- This results in a buildup of toxins, which poison the algae and the coral is bleached.
- Coral reefs are important to snorkelers, and divers.
- Marine life depends on coral reefs and may become extinct.
- It's a natural process but also caused by pollution and solar radiation.
- Coral can recover if sea temperatures become cooler.

B

1. The professor says that coral bleaching is occurring more often because sea temperatures are rising.
2. The professor gives snorkelers, divers, and marine life as reasons for why coral reefs are so important.

Page 89

D

The lecture is about coral.
A. Coral bleaching
   1. Coral is dying
   2. Temperature of the sea is rising
      - Coral bleaching is becoming more widespread
   3. Coral depends on algae for food and color
      - Toxins poison the algae
B. For over a hundred years sea temperatures have been rising and will continue to rise
C. Effects
   1. Fish and marine life may become extinct
   2. Tourism and fishing will lose income
Conclusion: Coral reefs are important and can be recovered if sea temperatures become cooler.

F

1. photosynthetic   2. elimination   3. prompts
4. prediction   5. exquisite

Page 90

Step 1

- Global climate is becoming warmer
- Predicted effects are rising sea levels and melting glaciers
- Melting ice kills marine life in colder regions
- Animals are in danger of becoming extinct
- Seventy frog species have become extinct
- Polar bears and seals depend on the cold

- Recently a polar bear drowned as it had no sea ice to rest on
- Rising sea levels results in the loss of beaches
- Animals and birds are affected
- People's homes will be destroyed and will have less drinking water
- To reduce the impacts of climate change we must change our habits fast

Step 3

The lecture is about how global climate is getting warmer.
A. Effects
   1. Melting ice sheets have caused the extinction of seventy species of frogs
   2. Polar bears and seals depend on the cold
B. Rising sea levels
   1. Beaches will be lost and animals and birds will die
   2. Homes will be destroyed and relocation will be expensive
   3. Drinking water will be destroyed by the sea water
C. Melting ice and rising sea levels are two of the effects of a warmer climate
Conclusion: A warmer climate will cause serious problems if habits are not changed.

Page 91

Step 4

The lecture is about the global climate getting warmer. Melting ice sheets can have serious consequences. For example, some frog species have become extinct and polar bears and seals depend on the cold. Rising sea levels mean the loss of many beaches, animals and birds, homes, and drinking water. Melting ice sheets and rising sea levels are two of the effects of the global climate getting warmer. We must change our habits fast to reduce the impacts.

Check-up

Page 92

1. bleaching   2. errands   3. marine
4. Precious   5. coral   6. picky
7. algae   8. snorkel
9. chores   10. hassle

[Unit 9]

Independent

Page 93

B

1. My father is a <u>TV broadcaster for sports games</u>.
2. The best part about my father's job is <u>the free tickets to all the big games</u>.
3. I wouldn't be interested in a job like my father's because <u>he has to travel a lot and doesn't get to spend a lot of time at home</u>.

Page 94

A

1. <u>I think that being a movie star would be really exciting</u>.
2. <u>The best part about the job would be all the money and the great clothes</u>.
3. <u>The worst part about the job would be the constant attention and all the photographers wanting to take my picture</u>.
4. <u>I wouldn't want to be a movie star because I don't like it when everyone looks at me</u>.

B

Doctor
Lawyer
CEO
Teacher
Scientist
Researcher
Pilot
Person in marketing
Negotiator
Diplomat
Professional athlete
Cowboy

C

What?	<u>Helping others</u> is very important to me.
Why?	It is important because <u>I am very lucky and I want to help others who are not so lucky</u>.
When?	A good example of this value was when <u>I volunteered to help teach poor children</u>.
How?	I try to use this value by <u>going every weekend to teach children who do not have much money</u>.

D

Something challenging
Honesty
Religious
Good reputation
Trust-worthy
Helping others
Being happy
Having lots of time with family
Being comfortable
Being rich

Page 95

F

Sample response 1

Challenging and stimulating

Reason 1
- Easy jobs become mundane
- Must do job everyday
- Boring job leads to boring life

Reason 2
- People who like their jobs think it is play
- Challenging jobs let you feel accomplished
- Feel proud at end of day

Conclusion: A challenging and stimulating job is what I want to have.

Sample response 2

Have great colleagues

Reason 1
- Spend lots of time at work so it is important to get along with colleagues
- Can make time go by quicker

Reason 2
- They are dependable
- Makes people work harder
- Can achieve more ambitious goals

Conclusion: Great colleagues can make a job great.

G

1. camaraderie   2. isolated   3. ambitious
4. attained   5. challenging

Page 96

Step 2

Sample response 1

Time with Family

Reason 1
- Hate feeling isolated
- Family makes feel like part of a group
- Everyone is looking out for each other

Reason 2
- Family is incredibly funny
- Never a boring or mundane moment
- Great sense of camaraderie

Conclusion: I must have a job that allows me to spend lots of time with my family.

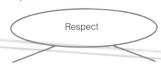

Sample response 2

Respect

Reason 1
- only attained with hard work
- challenging and stimulating
- other people look up and admire you

Reason 2
- have respect for self
- will be proud and continue to work hard

Conclusion: I must have a job that has a lot of respect.

Step 3

Sample response 1

I want a job that <u>gives me lots of time to be with my family</u>. This is so important because <u>I hate feeling isolated. My family makes me feel like I am a part of a big group. I feel that everyone is looking out for each other</u>. It's also important because <u>my family is incredibly funny. There is never a boring or mundane moment in our house. Everyone is always laughing and there is a great sense of camaraderie. If I were working all the time I would miss this</u>. I must have a job that <u>allows me to spend lots of time with my family</u>.

Sample response 2

I want a job that <u>has a lot of respect from other people</u>. This is so important because <u>jobs that have a lot of respect are only attained through hard work. They are challenging and incredibly stimulating. Other people look up to you and admire you for what you have done</u>. It is also important because <u>if I have one of these jobs, then I will have a lot of respect for myself. I will be very proud of my job and continue to work hard at it everyday</u>. I must have a job that <u>has a lot of respect</u>.

Integrated

Page 97

B
1. The university will <u>increase tuition at the beginning of next year</u>.
2. The university will increase tuition in order to <u>pay for programs and facilities for new students</u>.
3. I think the conversation will be about <u>the possible new programs and facilities</u>.

Page 98

B

Woman	Man
• Can't <u>believe it</u> • The increase seems small • But it's <u>substantial</u> • It will be <u>good for all the students at the university</u> • Already has <u>a lot of debt from university</u> • Will take <u>years to pay it all back</u> • Will have to <u>figure something out</u>	• Thinks it's <u>terrible</u> • Tuition is <u>too expensive for most students</u> • Couldn't <u>pay his tuition last year</u> • Had to <u>get a job</u> • Doesn't know <u>how he will afford to pay the increase</u> • Will have to <u>work more hours at his job</u> • Thinks they should <u>start a petition to stop the increase</u>

Page 99

D

The man thinks <u>the increase is bad</u>
A. Tuition
   1. Is <u>already too high</u>
B. He
   1. Couldn't <u>afford his tuition last year</u>
   2. Had <u>to get a job</u>
   3. Doesn't <u>know how he'll pay the increase</u>
   4. Will <u>have to work more hours</u>
C. He thinks the students should <u>start a petition to stop the increase</u>

F
1. accumulate   2. dean   3. maximum
4. supplementary   5. substantial

Page 100
Step 2

Man	Woman
• Received <u>a letter</u> • Has to <u>pay $25</u> or <u>he won't get his grade report</u> • Didn't know <u>about the fines being raised</u> • Thinks <u>it's awful</u> • Can't <u>afford to pay the higher fines</u> • Thinks it's unfair <u>to make students pay for the new computers</u> • Wishes <u>he had returned his books on time</u>	• Thinks it seems <u>like a lot of money</u> • Didn't know <u>fines were so expensive</u> • Remembers <u>a petition to increase fines</u> • Thinks <u>it's great</u> • The extra money <u>will make the computer lab better</u> • Strongly <u>supported the petition last fall</u> • Thinks it's unfair <u>when other students don't return their books on time</u> • Can't <u>get her research done</u> • Thinks <u>students who return books late should be punished</u>

Page 101
Step 4

The woman is <u>happy about the library fine increases</u>.

A. The woman
  1. supported <u>the petition for the increase</u>
  2. wants the extra <u>money to build a better computer lab</u>
B. She thinks
  1. it's unfair <u>when students return their books late</u>
  2. students <u>should be punished</u>

Step 5

The woman is <u>happy about the library fine increases</u>. She supported <u>the petition last fall</u> because she wants the extra <u>money for the new computer lab</u>. Also, she thinks it's unfair <u>when other students return their books late</u> and those students <u>should be punished</u>.

Check-up

Page 102

1. incredibly   2. student loan   3. mundane
4. awful   5. stimulating   6. effective
7. content   8. petition
9. pending   10. unity

[Unit 10]

Independent

Page 103

B

1. I think university students are <u>very independent and hard working</u>.
2. I think professors treat students <u>like adults with a greater sense of camaraderie</u>.
3. The most important lesson to learn at university is <u>how to take care of yourself</u>.

Page 104

A

1. <u>I have to brush my teeth every day</u>.
2. <u>I have to do this every day so that my teeth remain healthy and my breath smells good</u>.
3. <u>If I don't do this every day, my mouth feels really dirty and my breath smells bad</u>.
4. <u>I think I should have to do this every day because if I don't I won't feel good about myself</u>.

B

Studying hard
Cleaning your room
Taking care of a pet
Doing the dishes
Going to work
Helping your mom or dad
Babysitting or taking care of a younger sibling
Taking care of friends and family

C

What?   I had to <u>make my bed every morning</u>.
When?   I started to be able to choose to do this when <u>I got into middle school</u>.
How come?   I had to do this because <u>my mom told me that I had to do it</u>.
Why?   Now, I don't do this because <u>I hate making my bed, and think that it is a waste of time</u>.

D

Smoking
How to spend money
Go to school
When to go to bed
When to play with friends
How late to stay out with friends
What they want to eat

Page 105

F

Sample response 1

Reason 1
- University prepares students to be adults
- Students must be able to make decisions

Reason 2
- Many classes are seminars
- Have pre-made notes, large classes
- Have assistants lecturing
- Can get notes from friends

Conclusion: College students should not be obliged to go to class.

Sample response 2

Reason 1
- After university students get jobs
- Everyone goes to work every day
- Good practice for real world

Reason 2
- Goal of college is to get knowledge
- Learn by going to class
- Can have discourse with class

Conclusion: College students should be obliged to go to class.

G

1. predominant   2. discourse   3. obliged
4. ultimate   5. acknowledge

Answer Key

Page 106
Step 2
Sample response 1

Reason 1
- Hearing lectures lets you understand more
- Can ask questions
- Professors are there to ensure you can understand

Reason 2
- Shows respect for professors
- Going to class acknowledges them

Conclusion: Students should go to class every day.

Sample response 2

Reason 1
- Ultimate goal is to learn
- Can learn on their own if they want
- If they do well on exams, shouldn't have to go

Reason 2
- Students have other important things to do
- Some start businesses
- Attending business is more important than class

Conclusion: Students should not have to go to class every day.

Step 3
Sample response 1

College students <u>must</u> be obliged to go to class. Going to class <u>is</u> important because <u>having the professor lecture you will allow you to further your understanding by asking the professor questions. Topics at university are very complicated. Professors are there to ensure that students understand. They are also experts on the topics.</u> But the predominant reason is <u>that going to class shows respect for the professor. Professors are very accomplished people who deserve respect. Going to class acknowledges them.</u> Students should <u>go to class every day.</u>

Sample response 2

College students <u>mustn't</u> be obliged to go to class. Going to class <u>isn't</u> important because <u>the ultimate goal of university is to learn. A student can learn on their own if he or she so chooses. If the student never goes to class but still learns and does well on exams then there is no need to go to class.</u> But the predominant reason is <u>that many college students have other very important things that they are doing. Some college students find ways to start businesses. Attending to their businesses or important tasks is far more important than going to class.</u> Students should <u>not have to go to class every day.</u>

Page 107
B
1. The <u>microchip</u> was invented in Silicon Valley.
2. There are so many technology firms because <u>modern technology is reliant upon the microchip</u>.
3. I think this lecture will be about <u>how Silicon Valley started and what it is</u>.

Page 108
B

Location and name
- Is located <u>on the southern part of San Francisco Bay</u>
- Got its name from <u>two places, one from location, one from what was invented there</u>

What was started there
- Two Stanford graduates started <u>a computer company</u>
  - Name was <u>Hewlett-Packard</u>
  - Became <u>the biggest computer company in the world</u>
- Also worked on <u>the silicon microchip</u>
  - Robert Noyce and Gordon Moore started <u>Intel</u>
  - It was a <u>monumental invention</u>

What else came there
- People came because <u>all technology is reliant on the microchip</u>
- Needed <u>money and got it from venture capitalists</u>
- People became <u>really rich</u>

Page 109
D
The lecture and passage were about <u>Silicon Valley</u>.
A. Name
  1. Is located on <u>the southern part of San Francisco Bay</u>
  2. Got its name from <u>its location and what was invented there</u>
B. Companies
  1. Two Stanford graduates started <u>Hewlett-Packard</u>
    • It became the <u>biggest computer company in the world</u>
  2. Gordon Moore and Robert Noyce started <u>Intel</u>
    • Used the <u>microchip</u> to start their company
    • It was a <u>monumental invention</u>
C. New companies
  1. Companies soon came to Silicon Valley because <u>modern technology is reliant upon the microchip</u>
  2. These companies needed <u>money to grow</u>
  3. <u>Venture capitalists</u> gave them money
  4. People became <u>really rich</u>

F

1. inhabit   2. reliant   3. synonymous
4. federal   5. commerce

Page 110
Step 2

The second wave
- First in the second wave was <u>Apple</u>
- It raised <u>over one billion dollars from investors</u>

The 1990s
- Companies such as <u>Netscape, Yahoo, Adobe, Cisco, and Oracle all expanded</u>
- There was a <u>long period of economic growth</u>
- E-commerce started <u>to grow</u>
- Ebay, Google, and Verisign allowed <u>people to search, buy, and pay for items online</u>

The stock market
- American stock market became <u>reliant upon Silicon Valley</u>
- In 2000, <u>Silicon Valley went through a difficult time</u>
- This caused <u>a big decrease in the American stock market</u>

Silicon Valley now
- Now it is <u>doing well again</u>
- It is growing <u>into medicine</u>

Page 111
Step 4

The passage and the lecture were about <u>Silicon Valley</u>.

A. Companies
   1. Apple <u>was the first in the second wave; raised over one billion dollars</u>
   2. Adobe, Cisco, Netscape, Yahoo <u>all helped to lead to one of the longest periods of growth ever</u>
   3. Ebay, Google, Verisign <u>helped to start e-commerce, let you search, buy and pay for things online</u>

B. The American stock market became <u>reliant upon Silicon Valley</u>
   1. Silicon Valley helped to <u>lead to one of the greatest periods of growth</u>
   2. When Silicon Valley went down, <u>the entire stock market went down</u>

C. Now Silicon Valley <u>is doing well again</u>

D. The next great wave will be in <u>medicine</u>

Step 5

The passage and lecture were about <u>Silicon Valley</u>. Apple <u>was the first of the second wave of companies. It raised over one billion dollars from investors</u>. Adobe, Cisco, Netscape, and Yahoo all

<u>helped the American economy to go through one of the greatest expansions ever</u>. Ebay, Google, and Verisign then came along and <u>helped to start e-commerce. This allowed people to search, buy and pay for items all online</u>. The American stock market became <u>reliant upon Silicon Valley and its long period of expansion</u>. When it went down, <u>much of the stock market in America went down as well</u>. The next great wave in Silicon Valley will <u>most likely be in medicine</u>.

Check-up

Page 112

1. lecture   2. microchip   3. further
4. Pre-made   5. monumental   6. seminars
7. explode   8. assistant   9. venture capitalists
10. Silicon

[Unit 11]

Independent

Page 113

B

1. I have <u>a lot of family and friends in my hometown</u>.
2. I think there <u>aren't a lot of job opportunities</u> because <u>people always have to move to find a job</u>.
3. I think that it <u>is a great place to raise a family</u> because <u>it is very safe</u>.

Page 114

A

1. My father grew up in a different city.
2. He is very happy with moving to our city because he has a great job and a lot of really good friends.
3. My mom grew up in her hometown.
4. She is really happy living in our hometown because she lives close to her mom and can see all her family frequently.

B

Better universities
More urban feel
Want some solitude
Better job opportunities
Want a challenge
Was bored with hometown
Want a fresh start
Want something different
Doesn't like hometown

C

Which?	I visited <u>Jerusalem</u>.
When?	I visited <u>Jerusalem once ten years ago and another time five years</u> ago.
What?	The thing I liked most about this city was its <u>incredible sense of history and importance</u>.
Why?	I would want to live there because <u>it has a very religious and very important feeling to it</u>.

D

Very comfortable
Close to your family's heritage
Can be near friends
Easy to keep in touch with family
Understand the city well
Don't have to make new friends
Have a good support system
Easy life

Page 115

F

Sample response 1

Reasons
- Hard to keep in touch with family
- Can't cope with that
- Find new friends
- Family heritage is in hometown
- Would be in solitude

Examples
- Cousin moved to Europe
- Lived there for five years
- Moved home because he missed his family

Conclusion: The same thing would happen to me, so I'll live close to home.

Sample response 2

Reasons
- More challenges in an urban city
- Resentful of hometown people treating me like a child
- Want no preconceived ideas of who I am
- With technology you can keep in touch easily

Examples
- Two years ago moved to a new continent
- Love it
- Don't know when I'll go back

Conclusion: I like being far away from home.

G

1. urban   2. heritage   3. resentful
4. solitude   5. preconceived

Page 116

Step 2

Sample response 1

Reasons
- Worried going to be resentful when older
- No strain living in hometown
- Easy to keep in touch
- Will be disappointed when older

Examples
- Grandma encourages travel
- Lived in same city for eighty years
- Wishes she tried something new

Conclusion: I will follow her advice and move away soon.

Sample response 2

Reasons
- Get a good job, easy to cope with problems
- Lots of job opportunities in hometown
- Provide challenges and peers to work with
- This is more important than where you live

Examples
- Friend has a great job
- Moves every couple of years
- Is really happy
- Great to move around and meet new people

Conclusion: I will follow his example and find a great job, then find a good city.

Step 3

Sample response 1

I want to live <u>far away from home</u>. I want to do this because <u>I am worried that I am going to be resentful of not taking this opportunity when I am older. There is no strain living in my hometown. It is easy to keep in touch with my peers. It's comfortable now, but I am worried that I will be disappointed and resentful when I am older. For example, my grandma always encourages me to go traveling and to live somewhere else. She lived in the same city for eighty years. She wishes she had tried something new</u>. I will follow <u>her advice and move away soon</u>.

Sample response 2

I want to live <u>wherever I can get a good job</u>. I want to do this because <u>if I get a good job then it will be easy to cope with all the other problems. My hometown is very urban with a lot of job opportunities. A good job will provide you with good challenges and peers to work with. This is more important than where you live. For example, my friend has a great job. He moves around every couple of years. He loves his job and is really happy with his life. He says it's great to move around and meet new people. I will follow his example and find a great job, then find a good city</u>.

Page 117

B

1. The students are discussing <u>going to summer school or taking a vacation</u>.
2. The student's reasons for attending summer school <u>are that it would deduct from his workload next year and he could graduate early</u>.
3. I think the rest of the conversation <u>will be about which option will be the best for him</u>.
4. I think the student should <u>take a vacation over going to summer school</u>.

Page 118

A

Man	Woman
• Can't decide <u>between summer school and a vacation</u> • Will deduct <u>his workload for next year and he can graduate early</u> • Spoke <u>to the organizer</u> • Summer panel <u>of teachers are very energetic</u> • Can take <u>a long vacation if he graduates early</u> • Parents <u>have a radical trip planned</u> • Feels he can <u>graduate early enough to spend time with friends and go on vacation</u> • Still <u>has to decide</u>	• He deserves <u>a break</u> • Will perform <u>better if he takes a break from studying</u> • Impressed <u>by his trip</u> • Concerned <u>he won't spend time with his friends</u> • Says <u>he's putting himself under a lot of pressure</u>

B

1. The students discuss <u>that it will deduct from his workload next year. Then he could graduate early and go on vacation with parents and spend time with friends before university starts</u>.
2. The students discuss <u>that he worked hard and deserves a break. She also says it is implicit to take a break from studying so as to perform better in the exams</u>.

Page 119

D

The conversation is about <u>whether the student should attend summer school or take a vacation</u>.
A. Advantages of attending summer school
  1. Will <u>deduct from workload next year</u>
  2. Graduate <u>early and go to Europe with parents</u>
  3. Probable <u>that can go to Europe and still spend time with friends</u>
B. Advantages of taking vacation
  1. Studying <u>hard so it is implicit to take a break to perform better in exams</u>

2. Important <u>to spend time with friends before going away to university</u>
Conclusion: I think <u>he should take a vacation during the summer</u> because <u>it is important to rest and spend as much time with friends as possible</u>.

E

I think <u>he should attend summer school</u> because <u>his parents have promised to take him to Europe if he graduates early and it will also deduct from his workload next year</u>.

G

1. whereby   2. implicit   3. radical
4. deducts   5. panel

Page 120
Step 1

Woman	Man
• Hard-earned <u>trip as farm work is difficult</u> • Grades <u>are low so should go to summer school</u> • Improve <u>chance of getting into a good university</u> • Earn <u>little money as it will be deducted if he eats too much fruit</u> • Awesome <u>idea to make deal with parents whereby go to summer school and they pay for road trip</u>	• Grades <u>are low and parents say it is implicit to attend summer school</u> • Has a radical <u>job on a fruit farm</u> • Friend <u>organized road trip and was going to save to go with him</u> • Energetic <u>person so could do difficult work</u> • Great <u>working outdoors, blue skies, fresh air, and sun</u> • Probable <u>that he won't get university placement with his grades and could do with extra studying</u> • Maybe <u>he wouldn't save much money</u>

Step 3

The conversation is about <u>whether he should attend summer school or get a job</u>.
A. Planned to
  1. Get <u>a job working on a fruit farm</u>
  2. Save <u>money for road trip that friend organized for end of summer</u>
  3. Work <u>outdoors as would be great to have blue skies, fresh air, and sun</u>
B. Probable that <u>won't get a university placement with current grades</u>
C. Low grades
  1. Should <u>attend summer school to improve chance of a getting into a good university</u>
  2. Maybe <u>wouldn't save much money working</u>
  3. Could make <u>deal with parents whereby he goes to summer school and they pay for road trip</u>
Conclusion: I would prefer <u>to get a job and spend all of the vacation time outdoors enjoying good weather</u>.

Answer Key

The conversation is about <u>whether the student should attend summer school or get a job</u>. The student planned to <u>get a job and save for a road trip. He wanted to work outdoors and enjoy blue skies, fresh air, and the sun</u>. It's probable that <u>the student will not be offered a university placement as his current grades are low</u>. His grades are low <u>so maybe he should attend summer school to improve his chance of getting into a good university. He could make a deal with his parents whereby he goes to school and they pay for the road trip</u>. I would prefer to <u>attend summer school and try to improve my chance of getting into a good university</u>.

Check-up

Page 122

1. strain
2. keep in touch
3. cope
4. workload
5. organizer
6. perform
7. set
8. probable
9. awesome
10. peers

[Unit 12]

Independent

Page 123

B
1. My dad has had <u>three different</u> careers.
2. My dad has worked for <u>about five or six different companies</u>.
3. My dad has worked at his current job for <u>over eight years</u>.

Page 124

A
1. My dream job is to be a famous fashion designer.
2. At first, I want to work for a famous designer label to get experience and to learn how to be successful.
3. This is my dream job because I love fashion, and I love designing clothes.
4. I hope to be at this job for about ten years and then I want to start my own fashion label after I have some more experience.

B
Offered a promotion
Boring and mundane
Got fired
Changing marketplace
Make myself more employable
Attain new experiences
Try something new
Don't like my job

C
Who?   <u>My best friend's dad</u> changed jobs.
When?   He changed jobs <u>about a year ago</u>.
How come?   He changed jobs because <u>he was offered a big promotion at his new company</u>.
Why?   He is happy with the change because <u>he gets paid a lot more money, but he also has to work a lot harder</u>.

D
Continuity
Stability
Have a good relationship with peers
Family is relying on your job
It is easy
It is relaxing
Offered promotions in your company
Good retirement package
Good pay
Get a lot of respect from colleagues

Page 125

F
Sample response 1

> Change frequently

Reason 1
- World is rapidly changing
- Technology often changes
- Critical to have extensive skills and experiences

Reason 2
- Best way to get skill is through work
- Wide range of jobs will help get important skills

Conclusion: Frequently changing jobs helps people to be more employable later on in life.

Sample response 2

> Stay at same job

Reason 1
- Gives continuity and stability
- Others depend on income
- Makes sure family doesn't feel stressed

Reason 2
- Better chances for promotion
- Allows you to work at same place

Conclusion: Staying at the same job for a long time is what I want to do.

G
1. critical   2. continuity   3. promotion
4. attain   5. frequently

Page 126

Step 2

Sample response 1

Stay at same job

Reason 1
- Establish strong connections with peers
- Attain respect and admiration from peers

Reason 2
- Gives you and peers sense of continuity
- Critical for accomplishing your goals
- Ensures that you do the best quality work

Conclusion: It is much better to stay at the same job for a long time.

Sample response 2

Change when necessary

Reason 1
- When not happy, won't do good work
- If you like your job, stay
- If you don't like your job, change

Reason 2
- Stay on top of changing marketplace
- Can get critical start in important new areas

Conclusion: It is much better to change when you feel that you must.

Step 3

Sample response 1

I think people should stay at the same job for a long time. This is so important because staying at the same job allows you to establish strong connections with your peers. This allows you to attain their respect and admiration for you. More importantly, staying at the same job gives you and your peers a sense of continuity and stability. This is critical to accomplishing your goals. It also helps to ensure that you do the best quality work that you can. It is much better to stay at the same job for a long time.

Sample response 2

I think people should change jobs whenever they feel that it is necessary. This is so important because when a person doesn't feel happy any more, then they won't do his or her best work. People who like their jobs should stay there. People who don't like their jobs should do something new. More importantly, changing when it is necessary will ensure that you stay on top of the changing marketplace. It will allow you to get a critical start in important new areas that will let you be successful. It is much better to change when you feel that you must.

Integrated

Page 127

B
1. The lecture is mainly about the shows on Broadway.
2. Broadway was founded in the early 1900s.
3. I think the professor will talk about how Broadway has changed.

Page 128

A
- Broadway was founded in the 1900s
- In the beginning, shows provided light entertainment and bore no resemblance to real life
- Audiences were interested in music, excitement, romance and often became involved in the shows
- World War I Broadway supported soldiers by building theaters and raising money for the war
- Broadway began to deal more with social and political issues after the war
- Production grew dramatically
- Well known for its bright lights
- Great Depression in the 1930s caused the number of Broadway productions to fall
- Creative time for writers, who wrote about the American state of affairs
- Mass media was too much competition for Broadway
- But still an important aspect of American culture

B
1. The professor describes Broadway as light entertainment, which bore no resemblance to real life.
2. The professor discusses World War I, the Great Depression, and mass media as events and developments which brought changes to Broadway.

Page 129

D
The lecture is about Broadway.
A. Founded
   1. Shows provided light entertainment
   2. Bore no resemblance to real life
      • Audiences became involved in the shows
   3. Broadway supported the soldiers in World War I
      • Theaters were built to raise money for the war
B. After the war shows dealt with social and political issues and productions increased dramatically

Answer Key

C. 1930s
  1. Number of <u>shows dropped due to the Great Depression</u>
  2. Creative and <u>interesting time for writers</u>
Conclusion: Broadway responds to <u>changes in society and continues to be an important aspect of American culture</u>

F
1. prime   2. commercial   3. senselessness
4. dramatically   5. resemblance

Page 130
Step 1

• New York is <u>famous for many things such as Broadway</u>
• *Cats* is <u>one of the longest running Broadway musicals</u>
• Composed by <u>Andrew Lloyd Webber</u>
• Performed all around <u>the world and translated into many languages</u>
• Story is about <u>a tribe of cats who meet once a year to choose a cat to be reborn</u>
• *The Lion King* is <u>another popular musical, based on a Disney animated film</u>
• It is about <u>jealousy and evil and a father lion who dies and his son Simba becomes the Lion King</u>
• Musicals often use animals <u>to represent people in society</u>
• Theater is important <u>in people's lives all around the world</u>

Step 3

The lecture is about popular Broadway musicals.
A. *Cats*
  1. One of longest running <u>Broadway musical</u>
  2. First performed <u>in London, performed world wide and translated into many languages</u>
B. *The Lion King*
  1. Based on <u>a Disney animated film</u>
  2. Simba becomes <u>the Lion King</u>
  3. It is about <u>jealousy and evil</u>
C. Animals are used to <u>represent characters in society</u>
Conclusion: The theater is important to people, which is evident by the popularity of musicals performed all over the world.

Page 131
Step 4

The lecture is about <u>Broadway musicals</u>. *Cats* is one of the most famous musicals. It was <u>first performed in London, has been performed worldwide, and is translated into many languages</u>. *The Lion King* is

also a famous musical. It is about <u>evil and jealousy and a young lion who becomes the king</u>. Musicals are often written about <u>people in society</u>. People all over the world <u>enjoy the theater</u>.

Check-up
Page 132
1. employable   2. Mass media
3. stability   4. Broadway
5. state of affairs   6. extensive
7. globalized   8. production
9. bear   10. marketplace

[Review 2]

Independent 1
Page 133
Step 2
Sample response 1

Reason 1
- Moved to New Zealand
Like to
- Do adventure sports
- Spend time outdoors
Reason 2
- Lived on uncle's estate
Like to
- Horse ride
- Get to know cousins
Conclusion: Sometimes big changes can seem scary but can turn out to be great.

Sample response 2

Reason 1
- Joined drama society
Like to
- Meet new people
- Be creative
Reason 2
- Played leading role
Like to
- Sing and dance
- Wear beautiful costumes
Conclusion: Joining a club or trying a new activity can be more rewarding than you expect.

Step 3
Sample response 1

The best year of my life was <u>when my family moved to New Zealand</u>. At first, <u>I thought it would be the worst year of my life as I was moving from a city to live on my uncle's estate. I soon changed my mind because I got to ride horses and spend a lot of time outdoors. I also got to know my cousins better and the ultimate experience was being able to do so many adventure sports. Sometimes, big changes can seem scary but turn out to be great.</u>

Sample response 2

The best year of my life was <u>when I joined the local drama club</u>. At first, <u>I was nervous about joining a new club and trying something different. I soon realized how much I loved to sing and dance, be creative, and meet new people</u>. I also <u>got to wear a beautiful costume and play the leading role because the director said there was a resemblance between me and the character</u>. Sometimes, <u>trying something new can be more rewarding than you expected</u>.

Integrated 1

Page 134

Step 2

Russian Literature
- Before the <u>nineteenth century, very little Russian literature was read worldwide</u>.
- In the 1830s <u>it underwent a radical change</u>
- Resulted in <u>two of the most predominant novelists in literature, Tolstoy and Dostoevsky</u>

Dostoevsky
- *Crime and Punishment* <u>and Russian literature are synonymous with suffering</u>
- About a poor student <u>who kills a pawn broker for her money</u>
- Uses her money <u>to help a young girl take care of her family and he falls in love with her</u>
- She encourages <u>him to confess to the murder and she follows him to the city where his prison is</u>

Themes and popularity
- Themes frequently <u>deal with issues of modern concern, love, guilt, and religion</u>
- *Crime and Punishment* <u>has been translated into several languages and made into movies</u>

Page 135

Step 4

The passage and the lecture are about <u>Russian literature</u>.
A. Russian literature
 1. Has a long <u>and rich tradition but only read world wide since nineteenth century</u>
 2. Two of the <u>most predominant novelists in literature are Tolstoy and Dostoevsky</u>
 3. Dealt with <u>issues of modern concern, love, guilt, religion</u>
 4. Synonymous <u>with human suffering</u>
B. Dostoevsky
 1. Writer of <u>*Crime and Punishment*, which was translated into several languages</u>
 2. About a <u>man who kills a pawn broker for her money and helps a girl support her family</u>

 3. She encourages <u>him to confess to the police and she follows him to live near the prison</u>
 4. He believes <u>confession will put an end to his feelings of solitude</u>

Step 5

The passage and the lecture are about <u>Russian literature</u>. It has <u>a long tradition but only came to be read internationally since the nineteenth century</u>. Russia has produced <u>two of the most predominant novelists in literature. They are</u> Tolstoy and Dostoevsky. Russian literature at that time <u>dealt with issues of modern concern, love, guilt, and religion. It is synonymous with human suffering</u>. *Crime and Punishment* <u>was written by Dostoevsky. It has been translated into several languages and made into movies</u>. It is about <u>a man who kills a pawn broker for her money. He uses the money to help a girl to support her family. He falls in</u> <u>love with her and confesses to her. She encourages him to tell the police. He is sent away to prison and she follows him to live nearby</u>. The young <u>man confesses because he thinks it will put an end to his feelings of solitude</u>.

Integrated 2

Page 136

Step 1

Female Student	Male Student
• Dean suggested <u>she run for student president</u>	• How <u>can she concentrate on studies and run for president</u>
• Will be <u>challenging</u>	• Study <u>should be priority</u>
• All students <u>deviate from studies</u>	• Need <u>to modify schedule</u>
• Not <u>obliged to run for it yet</u>	• Advantages <u>are good on resume and meet exquisite people</u>
• Dean said <u>she is ambitious and would be good president</u>	• Take <u>a lot of time and effort to resolve issue</u>
• Think I <u>can cater to students' needs</u>	
• Own <u>work can not suffer because of it</u>	
• Good <u>camaraderie among candidates</u>	
• Resolve <u>major issues such as subordinate campus facilities</u>	
• Good <u>grades are critical to getting a good job and don't plan on career in politics</u>	

Step 3

The conversation is about <u>whether the female student should run for president or concentrate on her studies</u>.
A. The dean has <u>suggested she run for president as she is ambitious</u>
B. Reasons to run for president

Answer Key

1. Could cater <u>to students' needs and resolve subordinate on-campus facilities</u>
2. Look good on <u>resume and meet exquisite people</u>
3. Good <u>camaraderie amongst candidates</u>
C. Reasons to concentrate on studies
    1. Challenging <u>to concentrate on studies and run for student president</u>
    2. Own work <u>can not suffer because of it</u>
    3. Good grades <u>are critical to get a good job and doesn't plan a career in politics</u>
Conclusion: I would prefer <u>to run for student president because I think it would be a great experience and would look great on my resume.</u>

Page 137
Step 4

Example 1

The conversation is about <u>whether the student should run for student president or concentrate on her studies.</u> The dean <u>has suggested that she should run for student president. He said that she is ambitious and would make a good president.</u> She <u>thinks she could cater to students' needs and resolve the issue of the subordinate facilities on campus. She also thinks it would look good on her resume, and she will meet exquisite people.</u> However, <u>it will be challenging to concentrate on studies and run for president. It's important that her own work does not suffer. Good grades are critical to getting a good job, and she doesn't plan on a career in politics.</u> I would prefer <u>to run for student president because I think it would be a great experience. It would also look great on my resume and help me get a good job after university.</u>

I would prefer <u>to concentrate on my studies. I think that studying should be the main priority while at university. Good grades are necessary to get a good job.</u>

Page 138
Step 2

Sample response 1

Reason 1
- Need a break from studying
Better because
- Relax after school and exams
- Travel first as no time after university

Reason 2
- Need time to decide what to take at university
- Be sure of what course to take
- Be more mature starting university

Conclusion: It's important to take time off and travel.

Sample response 2

Reason 1
- Majority of students go to university
Better because
- Start at the same time as friends
- Not spend all of money traveling

Reason 2
- Better to go while still in study mode
- Hard to study after a long break
- More chance of finishing course if go straight from school to university

Conclusion: It's important to go to university right after school.

Step 3

Sample response 1

I think students <u>should take time off and travel after school.</u> Students <u>study hard to get into university, and it is important to take a long break and relax from studying before starting a university course.</u> It is important <u>to travel first as once university is over they will need to get a job. They will not have the time to travel.</u> I also think <u>that students need time to decide which courses are best suited to them. If they travel, they will be more mature when starting university.</u> It is more likely <u>that they will be sure about what they should study.</u> I would prefer <u>to travel after school and see some of the world before starting a job or university.</u>

Sample response 2

I think students <u>should go to university after school.</u> Students <u>usually go straight to university, and it's important to start at the same time as friends.</u> It is important <u>to have as much money as possible for university and traveling would be expensive.</u> I also think <u>that it is important to go to university while still in the study mode.</u> It is more likely <u>that students will find it difficult to study if they have taken a long break and have had so much freedom. They have a better chance of finishing their courses if they go straight from school.</u> I would prefer <u>to go straight from school with my friends. I would still have the opportunity to travel after university.</u>